Sharon L. Vanderlip, D.V.M.

Mice

Everything About History, Care,
Nutrition, Handling, and Behavior

Filled with Full-color Photographs
and Illustrations

BARRON'S

CONTENTS

INTRODUCTION TO THE MOUSE

Tiny and soft, bright eyed and dainty, the mouse has been a treasured pet and the focus of study for centuries. Of all the animals on this planet, it is certainly the best known. In ancient times the mouse was deified as an object of worship. Today it is respected for its invaluable contributions to medical science, and remains one of the world's most popular pets.

Our fascination with mice developed when we were children, from the time our parents read nursery rhymes and stories about mice to us. We learned songs and poems about mice in kindergarten. From the 1930s on, we were inundated with celebrity mouse animations in the movies, and later, on television. Walt Disney's Mickey Mouse has appeared in 119 animated short films plus a number of features, many with his companion, Minnie Mouse. Other Disney mouse heroes include Timothy Mouse, Dumbo the elephant's friend and coach; Cinderella's friends Gus and Jaq; Bernard and Miss Bianca of *The Rescuers Down Under*; and Basil in *The Great Mouse Detective*. In 1940 MGM introduced

Our fondness for the tiny, endearing mouse comes as no surprise. It was a friend of our childhood, in stories, songs, rhymes, and cinema. We have since learned that real mice are even more fun than their fictional characters!

Jerry Mouse, of *Tom and Jerry*, and Terrytoons followed with Mighty Mouse in 1942. Warner Brothers created Speedy Gonzales in 1953, and in the late 1950s Hanna-Barbera made several cartoons featuring mice, including Pixie and Dixie of *Huckleberry Hound*. More recently, 60 live trained mice and a computer-generated mouse starred in *Mouse Hunt* (1997). And no one can forget the three singing computerized puppet mice in *Babe*.

Our fondness for mice is certainly understandable. Yet, in spite of our familiarity with them, and their miniscule size, a wild mouse in the house can instill fear in some people as no other animal can. Why does a mouse evoke terror or attract affection and admiration? A close look at the history, biology, and lifestyle of mice and their relationship to humankind—all far more interesting than, and quite different from, the Hollywood versions—will put everything into proper perspective.

The mouse has a long and fascinating history, in which it plays a dual role. For thousands of years this tiny, unassuming animal has been the source of fear, myth, and reverence. Descriptions of the mouse range from varmint to beloved pet, and from culprit responsible for the spread of disease to biomedical hero as the ultimate research animal used to find medical cures. The small house mouse has a big story to share.

History of the Mouse

The word "mouse" is derived from the 4,000-year-old Sanskrit word "mush," meaning "to steal." Notorious for their ability to hide in granaries and homes and steal food, mice have played a major role in history. They have been responsible for serious losses of food, the spread of certain diseases, and even for victories and defeats in wars.

Throughout the World

The cat was deified in Egypt (around 2800 B.C., as the goddess Bastet) because of its ability to hunt and kill mice. Yet, as early as 1500 B.C., in the Middle East and the Orient, mice were protected and even worshipped. In fact, when warriors from Crete fought against the Troad of Asia Minor and won the battle, they credited their victory to mice! Reportedly, mice had chewed the leather from their opponents' shields, leaving them defenseless. As a token of their appreciation, the Greeks built a temple on the island of Tenedos in honor of the mouse god, Apollo smintheus. Mice were raised in the temple and used for healing arts and prophecy. The mouse god and the mice raised in the temple were held in such high esteem that they were represented on coins. The mouse god continued to be worshipped until the Turks conquered the area in 1453. (Mice have played a major role in more than one war: During World War II, field mice chewed up the wiring of German tanks hidden in fields. When called to action, only one-third of the tanks were operable and many of them short-circuited, failed, sparked, and even caught on fire on their way to the front lines.)

Throughout the Orient, the mouse was held in high regard as early as 1100 B.C., when Chinese priests used albino mice in religious rituals. The Chinese words for white mouse are "ancient one," dating back to the time of the first Chinese lexicon. In Japan, mice have been kept and raised in captivity since 80 B.C., when the Japanese documented the existence of mutant waltzing mice and also believed the mouse to be the messenger of the god of wealth.

Throughout the Orient, mice continue to be held in high regard. In China, one out of every twelve years is the "Year of the Mouse," with

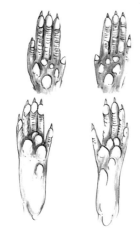

Mice have walking pads on the bottom of their feet that make it easier for them to run and climb over various surfaces.

11:00 A.M. to 1:00 P.M. considered to be the "Hours of the Mouse."

Medicinal Purposes and Scientific Research

From early Christian times to as late as the 1930s, mice were used for medicinal purposes—their body parts were blended with various oils, flowers, and other substances for use as potions to cure various ills.

Mice made their debut into scientific research in the early 1600s, when they were used in studies of anatomy, reproduction, and blood circulation. Mice have remained an important part of biomedical research ever since, and as the mouse gained popularity as a research model, it continued to earn its place in the animal lover's heart. In the field of biomedical research, more than 50 million mice are used worldwide every year, resulting in thousands of scientific publications. The mouse's major contribution to the advancement of medical science is the development of medical treatments for humans ranging from antibiotics to gene therapy. No animal has been studied as intensely, or has contributed as much to the human health field, as the mouse.

"Fancy Mice"

During the 1800s, mouse enthusiasts in Europe and Asia began exchanging mice of various colors and characteristics. They called these mice "fancy mice" and began raising and trading them. In addition to those highly

Scientists can tell a lot about mice from their teeth and the shape of their skull and use the information to categorize mice according to species and habitats.

prized for rare color mutations, mice with unusual traits or curious abnormalities have been bred and raised for centuries. For example, "waltzing" or "shaker" mice are defective in their balancing ability and shake, or appear to "waltz" about, instead of moving as normal mice do. "Singing mice" make faint but audible twittering sounds different from other mice. The proliferation of fancy mice contributed to the tremendous increase and interest in mouse experimentation, particularly in the area of genetics.

The ancient, popular hobby of mouse breeding has lasted to this day. As we enter the twenty-first century, mice continue to rank among the most favorite and interesting of "pocket pets" (a term of endearment for pets small enough to fit into your pocket).

Mouse Characteristics

"House mouse" is a general term encompassing several species of mice known to live in close proximity to humans and their homes. *Mus muscularis* and *Mus domesticus* are native to Western Europe and North America, but can be found throughout the world today. There are several subspecies of mice and they are grouped according to specific characteristics of their skull, teeth, bodies, measurements, and natural habits.

The cat was considered a god in Egypt because it hunted and killed mice, and special breeds of dogs have been bred to kill rodents. Although your pets may seem gentle, don't take chances! Never leave your mouse within reach of other animals.

Mice need space to play and explore. The size of cage you select will depend on the number of mice you decide to keep.

Because their eyes are very sensitive to light, mice should always have a dark place to hide. Bright light can cause pain and eye damage in mice.

Born hairless and weighing only .035 ounce (1 g) at birth, a mouse can gain up to 1½ ounces (42.5 g) or more, depending on the species, by the time it is fully grown. A mouse can reach sexual maturity as early as six weeks of age. From the tip of its nose to the end of its rump, the tiny creature measures only 2.5 to 3.7 inches (65–95 mm), depending on its strain (genetic background), as an adult.

✔ The mouse's endearing appearance is partly attributable to its bright eyes, rounded ears, and small nose.

✔ There are two main types of hair on the mouse: pelage (outer and undercoat) and tactile hairs (whiskers).

✔ Long whiskers (vibrissae) grow in rows along the snout and upper lip, a small group of long whiskers is located above the eyes, one long whisker is found below the eyes, and short whiskers are located under the chin.

✔ Mice come in a wide variety of colors and patterns, including brown, black, gray, beige, and albino.

✔ There is a small cleft in the upper lip, exposing the upper incisors (front teeth).

✔ All four feet have five digits each, although the first digit on the front feet (the "thumb")

is short and appears only as a flattened nail. Walking pads, as well as sweat glands, are located on the bottom of the feet.

✔ The tail is long and appears to be naked, although it is actually covered with fine hairs.

Anatomy

Eyes: Mice may have dark eyes or red eyes, depending on their genetics. They have poor eyesight and are sensitive to bright light. They rely primarily on their senses of hearing, smell, and touch.

Ears: Mice have a keen sense of hearing and rely on their auditory senses to listen for approaching danger and distress calls of other mice. Hearing is not well developed until 11 days of age. Mice can hear and communicate in ultrasonic ranges. They can hear sounds ranging from 80 Hz to 100 kHz and are most sensitive at 15 kHz to 20 kHz and 50 kHz. Hearing ability in mice varies with their age and genetic strain. Their large ears

No animal has been studied as much, or has contributed as much to medical research, as the mouse.

Adult Mouse Measurements

Weight	Length of Head and Body	Length of Tail
1/4–1 ounce (7–28 g)	2.5–3.7 inches (65–95 mm)	2.3–4 inches (60–105 mm)

Mouse Dental Formula

$$i\ 1/1,\ c\ 0/0,\ p\ 0/0,\ m\ 3/3 = 16$$

The number above the slash represents one-half of the upper jaw (left or right side), and the number under the slash represents one-half of the bottom jaw (left or right side).

i = incisors
c = canine teeth
p = premolars
m = molars

For example, there is one incisor in the upper jaw on the right side and one incisor in the right side of the lower jaw. There are no canine teeth or premolars in the mouth. There are three molars in the right side of the upper jaw and three opposing molars in the right side of the lower jaw for a total of eight teeth. Multiply eight by two, to include all the teeth on the left side of the mouth, and the total number of teeth equals sixteen.

serve to capture and direct sounds and to dissipate body heat.

Nose: Although mice have small noses, their sense of smell (olfaction) is very keen and plays an important part in their social life. Odors and scent marking are forms of communication used by mice to stake out territory and recognize other mice in the colony.

Body: Mice are tiny and agile. They are able to squeeze into the smallest of spaces in an effort to escape danger or hide.

Legs and feet: Mice legs and feet may be delicate, but they are surprisingly powerful for the animal's small size. Mice can jump, run quickly, and climb with ease.

Tail: Mice have long, sturdy tails for their size. The tail is very sensitive to pain. However, mice can be picked up by the midsection of the tail without causing discomfort, if they are handled gently. The tail serves as a balancing aid for the mouse, as well as an important means of dissipating heat. If the tail is injured and separates from the body, the missing portion of the tail will not grow back.

Because their teeth grow continuously throughout life, mice require safe chew sticks to keep their teeth worn correctly.

Mouse Biology

Natural habitat	Forests, savannahs, grasslands, fields, shrubby terrain, rocky areas, burrows, cultivated fields, and human habitations.
Number of chromosomes	40 (20 chromosome pairs).
Natural illnesses	Cancer, tumors.
Body temperature	99.5°F (37.5°C).
Heart rate	310–840 beats per minute. 570 beats per minute at rest.
Respiratory rate	150–180 breaths per minute.
Metabolic rate	Mice have a high metabolic rate due to the large number of circulatory, respiratory, and metabolic functions they must perform every minute and because of their large surface area to body mass. The metabolic rate of a mouse that weighs 1 ounce (28 g) is 13 times that of a 1,000-pound (445-kg) horse per gram of body tissue.
Food consumption	Approximately ½ ounce per 3–4 ounces of body weight, or ⅙ ounce of food per mouse per day (15 g per 100 g of body weight, or 6–7 g of food per mouse per day).
Water consumption	½ ounce per 3–4 ounces of body weight, or ⅙–⅓ ounce per mouse per day (15 ml per 100 g of body weight, or 4–10 ml per mouse per day).
Urine excretion	⅟₆₀–⅟₃₀ ounce per mouse per day (½–1 ml per mouse per day).
Sensitivities to change in temperatures	Low tolerance to heat, will die at 98.6°F (37°C). If temperature change is sudden, can die at 78°F (25.5°C). Mice do not salivate or pant to cool. Mice require several weeks to acclimate to cold weather.
Poor eyesight	Albinos and colored mice have very poor eyesight and are sensitive to light.

Teeth: Mice have 16 teeth, consisting of two upper and two lower front teeth (incisors) and 12 molars (three molars on each side, upper and lower jaws). There is a large space between the incisors and the molars, called the diastema.

Special anatomical features: In the female, there are three pairs of nipples in the pectoral region (chest) and two pairs in the inguino-abdominal region. The nipples are not usually visible except in infant mice, or pregnant or lactating females. The mammary tissue extends as far dorsal as the shoulder blades along the length of the trunk and can be confused with mammary tumors, which are common in mice.

The female mouse's uterus is bicornate, (meaning the uterus is Y-shaped and branches

Their noses may be small, but their sense of smell is keen! The large ears and long tails help keep mice cool by dissipating heat.

A mouse's eyes can be bigger than its stomach! A little bit of cheese is fine, but don't overdo it!

Mice need a lot of water to fuel their fast metabolism. Make sure your mice always have plenty of fresh water available.

The Egyptian spiny mouse is one of more than 1,000 close relatives of the domestic mouse.

A mouse will wash its face several times a day. Mice learn to groom themselves and wash their faces at a very young age, before weaning.

Mice love to nap, especially during the day. Give your pet lots of nesting material and try not to startle it while it is sleeping. Disturbed mice can wake up irritable and may bite!

Mouse Facts

Scientific name	*Mus musculus, Mus domesticus.*
Origin	Western Europe and Asia.
Color	Wide variety of colors, including white, brown, black, gray, beige, and albino.
Behavior	Active, territorial, colonial, sociable.
Lifestyle	Opportunistic and adaptable, living in areas close to human habitation, including houses, barns, or in fields and burrows.
Life span	Short-lived, one to three years.

into two parts). These two elongated parts of the uterus, called uterine horns, make it easier for the mouse to carry and give birth to several young.

Mice have a genetic makeup of 20 chromosome pairs (40 chromosomes).

What Makes Mice Rodents?

Mice are rodents. Rodents are among the most diverse and numerous of mammalian species. They are remarkably uniform in structural characteristics. All rodents have four incisors, two upper and two lower. These front teeth grow throughout life, continuously being pushed up from the bottom of the jaw, to

compensate for the continual wear they receive from biting hard objects. There are no nerves in the front teeth, except at the base where they grow, and continual wear of the incisors maintains very sharp cutting surfaces. Rodents do not have canine teeth or anterior premolars, so there is a rather large space between the front teeth and the cheek teeth. The cheek teeth are used for grinding and may have many peculiar patterns. These dental patterns, as well as jaw structure, are useful to zoologists and paleontologists for determining how different rodent species developed over time, their relationship to each other, and their origin.

Rodents are classified according to anatomical characteristics, similarities in teeth and bone structure, origin, and lifestyle.

Mouse Taxonomy

Kingdom Animalia
  Phylum Chordata
    Class Mammalia
      Order Rodentia
        Suborder Myomorpha
          Family Muridae
            Genus *Mus*
              Species *Mus musculus,*
                Mus domesticus

Their Place in Nature

Animals, insects, and plants are classified and grouped according to their differences and similarities. Names are assigned according to kingdom, phylum, class, order, family, genus, and species. With each progressive category, animals grouped together are more closely related. For example, all animals are part of the Kingdom Animalia, but only rodents are members of the Order Rodentia. The name given to a class, order, family, genus, or species may come from different sources. Animals can be named according to a special characteristic of their group, named after the person who discovered them, or even named after the geographical area they naturally inhabit.

Mouse Classification

The mouse is a member of the Kingdom Animalia (Animal Kingdom), the Phylum Chordata (animals having spinal columns), and the Class Mammalia (mammals). The word *mammalia* refers to the mammary glands (mammae, teats, or breasts). Newborn and baby mammals are nourished by milk from their mothers' breasts. All warm-blooded animals with hair or fur have mammary glands and belong to the Class Mammalia.

Order Rodentia: The word Rodentia is derived from the Latin word *rodere*, which means "to gnaw." This refers to a rodent's need to constantly chew on hard objects to keep the teeth from growing too long. The most important characteristic shared by all rodents is the continual growth of their front teeth throughout their entire lives. Within the Order Rodentia, there are three suborders. Mice are grouped in the Suborder Myomorpha.

Family: Rodents may be further classified into more closely related groups called families. There are 29 Recent rodent families. The mouse belongs to the Muridae family, which is by far the largest mammalian family, containing 267 Recent genera and 1,138 species.

Genus and species: Families are further divided into genera, a collection of even more closely related animals. There are 426 rodent genera. Mice are members of the *Mus* genus. There are 4 subgenera and 40 species of mice. The species of mice that concern us in this book are *Mus domesticus* and *Mus musculus*. Although mouse taxonomy may change with additional scientific investigation, based on biochemical and genetic studies, *Mus domesticus* is currently generally recognized to be a subspecies of *Mus musculus*.

Of the 1,814 species of rodents in existence today, none has been studied more intensely or is more intriguing and historically influential than the mouse.

BEFORE YOU BUY

Mice make wonderful pets for children and adults alike. They are fun to watch, inexpensive to maintain, and take up very little space. But just because mice are small doesn't mean there isn't a lot to consider before you can add one to your family. Responsible pet ownership always involves a certain amount of planning, commitment, time, and expense. In all fairness to yourself and your future pet, always do your homework first and learn as much as possible about the animal, its requirements, its health, and its behavior.

Special Considerations

Mice are delightful, active animals that love to explore. They are fascinating to watch, and when handled gently and regularly, are fun to hold. Mice are very easy to maintain in captivity. But be careful! They are tiny, quick, and nimble—a sure combination that can lead to escape or injury. So, if you prefer to simply relax and watch these inquisitive creatures at play, that's fine, too. Mice are great entertainers.

Now that you have fallen in love with mice, you want to know whether one or more of these small animals will be compatible with your lifestyle before you bring it home. Here are some considerations to help you decide.

Mice are easy to please. A small basket makes a cozy home for a busy mouse— while it lasts! Mice love to chew up their houses, so be ready with a replacement when one is needed.

Your Lifestyle

You and your family are the first consideration. How you live, and what you do, are important factors in assessing how well a mouse will fit into your lifestyle. The addition of a new pet should be nothing less than a happy and positive experience for you and the other members of your family.

It has been well documented that pet ownership has many benefits. People who own animals have been known to derive certain physiological and psychological benefits from the human-animal bond they form. Pet owners feel wanted and needed, and indeed they are; after all, their animals depend on them for food and care, and give friendship in return. Caressing or holding an animal has been shown to reduce blood pressure in some cases. Recent medical research suggests that people who own pets may even live longer!

But pet ownership is not always easy. In addition to time and money commitments, there is the sadness that accompanies the eventual illness, loss, or death of an animal friend. Naturally, the longer you have a pet, the more attached to it you become. Because mice have very short life spans, you must be prepared for the inevitable loss of your pet. You may decide to always keep more than one mouse at a time to ease the sense of loss that you will experience when one of your mice dies.

Some people can develop serious allergies to mouse urine or dander or animal bedding material. If you have allergies to pets or pet dander, or if you have a compromised immune system, be sure to consult your physician before obtaining a pet of any kind.

Cost

The purchase price of a mouse is minimal compared to the costs involved in time, housing, food, space, toys, and veterinary care. Fortunately, mice don't eat a lot and their food is relatively inexpensive, as are the wide variety of toys you can make for your mice. Your biggest expense will be housing, in the form of a cage or a Plexiglas aquarium, and bedding material. Mice require a minimal amount of time to feed and clean so most of your time can be spent enjoying and observing your pet.

Time

Mice are not demanding pets and they do not require a great deal of your time. The number of mice you own and the size of their cage will determine how often you will need to clean the cage (see Accommodations for Your Mouse, page 37). Most cages do not need to be cleaned more than once a week. Fresh water and food must be provided daily (see Feeding

Your Mouse, page 57). If you want to be able to hold and pet your mouse, be sure to take a few minutes each day to handle it. This contact is important to keep your mouse tame. Mice enjoy interacting with their owners and exploring. While you are holding your mouse, check it over thoroughly to be sure it is healthy and doing well. Visiting, handling, feeding, and watering take only a few minutes a day—a small investment to ensure that your bright-eyed companion is healthy and content.

Materials

Mice do require a few basic essentials:
✔ safe, comfortable, escape-proof housing with a secure door or lid
✔ nutritious food
✔ appropriate bedding material
✔ a water bottle
✔ a nest box or hiding place
✔ chew toys

Your mouse especially needs plenty of exercise. This is easy to provide in the form of an exercise wheel. An exercise wheel is not only a toy, it is a necessity. Ideally, the exercise wheel you purchase should have a solid floor, rather than rungs. This will prevent your pet from accidentally being caught and injured between the rungs of the wheel or from developing sores on its feet.

Mice enjoy any toys or activities that make life more interesting. Favorite mouse playthings include chew sticks, tunnel tubes, ramps and branches to climb, and hideaways. You can make many mouse toys yourself, such as inexpensive tunnels from PVC plumbing pipe from your local hardware store, wooden nest boxes and hiding places from untreated, nontoxic wood, and branches from nonpoisonous plants.

Scientific research has shown that mice that have more toys also have more neurons in the hippocampus of their brains!

Space

Mice don't require a lot of space, but they should have enough room to play, run, climb, and explore. Of course, the more mice you house together, the greater the cage space they will require (see minimum cage size requirements in Accommodations for Your Mouse, page 39).

Location: Finding just the right location for your pets' cage is important. It must be out of direct sunlight, especially if part of the cage is made of glass or Plexiglas. Even if the temperature within your home is comfortable, a solid-walled cage placed in direct sunlight can heat up rapidly, just like a greenhouse. The inside of the cage can become extremely hot and your mice could die from heatstroke. It is also important to place the cage in an area away from cold and drafts so your mice do not become chilled and develop pneumonia. This is especially important to protect the health of baby mice.

Finally, try to place the cage at a comfortable level for viewing and handling. Ideally, you will want to find a location where you can enjoy the animals' activities and be able to reach in to catch them or feed them, clean the cage, change the water bottle, and replace the bedding without having to bend over or stoop.

Other Household Pets

One of the biggest threats to a mouse is the presence of another animal. Mice have a very

Do not allow other household pets near your mouse where they can harm it.

keen sense of smell. They know when there are other animals in the house. Your mice will become stressed or frightened if your other pets come near the cage. Make sure the lid or door to the cage is securely fastened. Be sure to place the cage well out of reach of the family dog, cat, ferret, bird, or any other pet. You probably never thought of your house pets as being harmful, but cats and ferrets are natural

hunters and dogs can play rough. Even birds can quickly peck a small rodent to death. And large pet reptiles would find your mouse to be the ideal size for a meal. Although a mouse can inflict bite wounds when frightened, it is certainly no match for these animals.

For the safety of all the pets in your household, keep your mice well isolated.

Daily handling will help keep your pet tame and gentle.

Children

For everyone's viewing enjoyment, you will want to place your pets' cage where its activities can be easily observed. Inquisitive small children are naturally drawn to animals and interesting cages and containers. Unfortunately, small children can also accidentally drop a tiny animal, leading to possible injury, escape, or loss. Children should be supervised at all times while watching or handling a mouse. To prevent injury to your pet, and heartbreak to the child, be sure to teach children in the household how to correctly and gently pick up and handle a mouse. Your mouse may be calm around you and easy for you to handle, but a stranger's voice, or a child's sudden movements, may startle it. If your mouse is frightened, it may bite or try to escape. It can slip out of small hands in a heartbeat, but it may require hours to capture it, assuming you are lucky enough to do so. The safety of the child and your pet is your responsibility. When you cannot be there to supervise their activity, place the mouse cage out of the reach of small children. This is a safety measure well worth the temporary inconvenience.

Nocturnal Activities

In the wild, mice are most active at night (nocturnal). Domestic mice are active during the day and night. They take naps throughout the day. In addition, their day and night activity levels can be influenced by outside factors.

Young children should always have adult supervision when they play with mice.

Veterinary Care

Mice are generally hardy animals that do very well with good care and nutrition. However, if one of your mice becomes sick or injured, you may need to take it to your veterinarian for an examination and possible treatment. It is important to determine the cause of illness to be sure that the problem is not contagious to you or your other pets.

Mouse medicine is a very specialized field. Realistically, it is targeted at colony health rather than individual health. This is because it is difficult, expensive, and often unsuccessful to undertake heroic measures to save an individual mouse when it is very sick. However, by knowing the cause of illness, you can often take preventive measures to stop the problem before it spreads to other mice in the colony.

Many veterinarians specialize in pocket pets, or have a special interest in these small animals. Pocket pets have nutritional, housing, and medical requirements that are very different from the larger companion animals. They can be sensitive to certain products and medications used for treating more common pets.

When to Acquire a New Pet

Although you may want a mouse right now, today might not be the best time to buy your pet. If you have several obligations and your free time

Rats may be cute rodent cousins to mice, but they are also natural predators of mice. To avoid stressing your mice, house your pet rats in a separate room, away from your mice.

If your pet doesn't seem to be itself, contact a veterinarian who has a special interest in pocket pets.

is limited, you may want to postpone buying your mouse until you have more time to enjoy it. For example, if you are moving or changing jobs, a new pet may be added stress rather than enjoyment. If the holidays are approaching, it would be best to wait until later when you will have the time to relax and enjoy your pet without the hustle, bustle, and confusion of visitors and deadlines. If you are planning a vacation soon, you can avoid having to make arrangements for animal care in your absence if you wait until you return before you purchase your pet.

Selecting Your Mouse

Where to Find a Mouse

Mice are easy to find. They may be purchased from virtually any pet shop (listed in your telephone book), as well as from mouse breeders and hobbyists who advertise in pet magazines (available in bookstores and pet shops), local newspapers, or on the Internet. Your veterinarian may also know some mouse breeders or mouse clubs you can contact.

How to Select Your Mouse

If possible, look at as many mice as you can before you make a selection so that you can compare the overall health and quality of the animals, the cleanliness of their environment, and the variety of colors available.

✔ It is best to purchase a very young mouse, or a mouse that has been recently weaned. Remember that mice have a short life span, so the younger the mouse, the more time you will have to enjoy its companionship.

✔ Young mice are smaller and more active than older mice. Their coats are shinier and in better condition.

✔ An old mouse may appear ruffled, slower, and less alert.

✔ An older mouse will be difficult to introduce to your mouse colony; it will tend to fight with the others. If you purchase weanling mice, they should be able to integrate and socialize with minimal fighting.

Once you have chosen a mouse to take home, ask if you can pick it up and hold it before you buy it. You will quickly learn how tame the mouse is by how well it behaves when you handle it. If it tries to bite, continue your search for a less frightened and more socialized individual.

If the mouse you have selected is tame and allows you to handle it gently, examine it closely to be sure it is in good health. Are the eyes bright and clear? Is the coat smooth and well groomed? Does the skin look healthy and free of parasites? If possible, examine the front teeth to make sure they are properly aligned in the mouth. The teeth are naturally a dark yellowish orange color.

The mice you finally select will depend on their age, health, physical attributes, and your personal color preferences. Try to obtain weanling mice from the same litter, so that they will be compatible. Do not house male mice together. Your new mice should have a minimum of five days to acclimate to their new surroundings and should be kept isolated for ten days to two weeks from other mice you may have.

Before you introduce your new mice into a cage containing strange mice, clean the cage and replace the bedding. This way your established mice will not perceive the new mice as intruders into their home cage or be as likely to fight with them

Do not house male mice together. They are aggressive and will fight to the death. Do not purchase older mice. They also tend to fight with other mice in the established colony.

because the clean cage will no longer contain their own scent.

Aggression: Observe your mice closely for any signs of aggression. Your mice will establish a hierarchy, or pecking order, based on age, sex, and reproductive condition. Once the animals have settled down together peacefully, do not keep changing animal groups. This is very stressful for the animals and stimulates fighting. Keep your compatible groups the same!

How Many Mice to Keep

If you simply want an interesting companion in your home, one mouse can certainly fill the bill. One mouse can provide a surprising amount of company. However, in all fairness to your pet, remember that mice are very colonial animals. They do best when they can interact with members of their own species. They enjoy group housing and socialization. For these reasons, you should consider keeping a minimum of two mice, ideally two compatible females—unless you plan on raising mice, in which case you would purchase a male and a female. Keeping more than one mouse is a good thing for you, too. It is always a comfort to have a mouse to cheer you up if the other one should die.

If you are thinking about raising mice as a hobby, you will need to buy at least one pair of mice. In this case, you will want to find one or more reputable mouse breeders. An experienced mouse breeder can

In male mice, the distance from the anus to the urethral orifice is greater than in female mice.

be a valuable source of information and answer many questions about mouse behavior, resources, and coat color genetics. A mouse breeder can provide information about rodent or pocket pet clubs in your area. Also, clubs are a great way to meet other people who share your interest in these fascinating animals.

How many mice you own is strictly up to you. Mice should be fun. You never want to have so many animals that it seems you spend more time cleaning up after them than enjoying them. Keep your animal numbers reasonable so that most of the time you spend with your mice will be fun time. The number of mice you keep all depends on your lifestyle, how much housing space you can provide, and the amount of time you can dedicate to these charming creatures.

Male or Female?

The decision about whether to acquire a male or a female mouse will depend on your reasons for buying a mouse. If you are simply

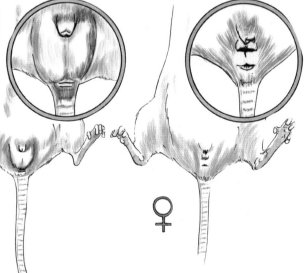

Be sure to buy a young mouse that is recently weaned, like the youngster on the left. It will be gentler and easier to tame.

Mice rely heavily on their keen sense of smell to inform them of their surroundings. They like to climb on things and stand up to better sniff the air.

Fresh fruits (in moderation!) make healthy treats for active mice.

Mice are very social animals and enjoy each other's company.

If you decide to keep more than one mouse, you won't be disappointed. It's fun to watch their antics and comical play behavior.

Children and adults can learn a lot about biology and genetics from raising mice. The silky, longhair characteristic is an inherited trait that produces an unusual and attractive mouse.

looking for a great pet and an interesting companion, you will be happy with either a male or female mouse. If you are planning to raise mice, however, you will obviously need at least one pair to begin your project.

The main physical difference you will note is the presence of the scrotum in the male mouse. The main behavioral differences will be the male's tendency to urinate more frequently, as a way of scent-marking his territory (see Understanding Your Mouse, page 29). Don't worry. As long as your pets' cage and bedding are clean, there should be no offensive odors. If you can smell the mouse urine, it is past time to clean the cage!

Age and Longevity

The ideal age to bring your new mouse home is when it is recently weaned and no longer needs its mother for nutrition, warmth, and protection. There are two good reasons to buy a young mouse rather than an older one. First, a baby mouse is gentler and easier to handle and tame. A baby will adapt quickly to you and its new home. Second, mice have very short life spans. The sooner you acquire your mouse, the more time you will have to share with it and enjoy it.

How long do mice live? The life span will vary with each individual animal and the care and nutrition it receives. On average, mice can live one to three years. During this short time you will no doubt develop a strong emotional attachment to your endearing pet and when it dies you will experience the heartache that accompanies such a loss. On the positive side, mouse ownership does not impose a long-term commitment, as with a dog that may live to be 16 years old, or a parrot that can live 50 years!

If you already know you want mice to be a part of your life for several years, you may wish to always keep two or more mice at a time. Having more than one mouse will help ease the pain and fill the void when a mouse eventually dies.

Children and Mice

Mice make interesting and educational pets for children. Very young children must learn, however, that it is safer to observe mice in their cages rather than attempt to hold them because they are so small they are easy to crush or injure. Mice are also escape artists.

Safety First

The first thing children should learn about any pet is to not put their face up close against the animal. It is very tempting to rub a cheek across the soft fur, or even try to kiss the animal. But be sure to teach children from the very beginning that this is the one thing they must not do. The majority of all animal bite wounds inflicted on children—regardless of animal species—happen in the area of the face and head. Children should also learn to wash their hands thoroughly after handling any pets, especially before eating.

Teaching Responsibility

With adult guidance, there is no limit to the things children can learn from a pet mouse. Mouse ownership provides an excellent opportunity for adults to teach children about pets, the importance of humane care and treatment, and respect for life. Mice make wonderful school science projects. They can be the focus of study for topics such as animal behavior, exercise, nutrition, color genetics, or reproduction.

A mouse in the house is a great way for very young children to learn to be responsible. They can participate in the mouse's care and learn about the importance of fresh water, good food, and a clean home. Older children can learn a lot about animal behavior and biology, simply by observing. It is amazing to watch how dedicated mouse parents are while they raise their family.

Adult Supervision

Some children are uncomfortable around animals, especially large animals. Because a mouse is small, it can make it possible for a child to replace anxiety, fear, or timidity with tenderness and affection. But remember, adult supervision is necessary when a child is handling a mouse. Supervision prevents accidental bite injuries to the child and accidental escape by or injury to the mouse.

Even children who are somewhat shy will often talk freely when they are in the presence of animals. A small mouse can play a big part in opening doors of communication and learning for a child. While sitting still and observing such a fascinating animal, a child becomes a captive audience and a good learner. Together, you and your child can share thoughts and ideas about animals, people, families, and anything else you can relate to mice and humans on the child's level.

Animal Life and Death

Even with the best possible care, mice eventually become ill or die. Because mice have a relatively short life span, they do not require a long-term commitment from you. Although you may use mice to teach children in your family responsibility, in reality, you are the person ultimately responsible for the animal's care and well-being. Make sure that you share as much, or more, interest in the mouse as the child does. Remember that children's interests naturally change. It would be unreasonable not to expect a child's interest in mice to eventually dwindle over time. So be prepared for that day when you might be solely responsible for the mouse's care. On the other hand, a child can be quite enamored with a small rodent friend and remain attentive to the animal for its entire life.

Children are very sensitive to issues of animal life and death. The death of a mouse may seem trivial to some individuals, but it can be a tremendous loss to a child, especially if it is the first loss the child experiences. It is very important that the child be prepared in advance for the eventual, and inevitable, loss or death of any beloved pet. It is especially important that this preparation be provided in a compassionate manner appropriate for the child's age and level of maturity. The loss of a pet can be a very emotional experience for a child, but if handled skillfully, this loss can be turned into a positive learning experience. It provides an opportunity in which you may openly discuss life, love, illness, or death and possibly address additional fears or concerns the child may have. A tiny mouse can play a big role in helping a child grow, mature, and strengthen in character.

UNDERSTANDING YOUR MOUSE

The mouse's success as a species and its ability to survive in the wild are due to its communal lifestyle, rapid development, and ability to produce large numbers of offspring at an early age. Domesticated mice retain all the attributes of their wild cousin counterparts. Their behavior, adaptability, and survival strategies have been shaped and influenced by the selective forces of their numerous predators.

For thousands of years, wild mice have adapted to living in close proximity to humans. From fields to houses, above ground or below, mice have set up housekeeping in almost every conceivable kind of environment. Mice are inquisitive, yet wary, and stay close to the safety of their homes. They sleep a lot and exit their nests when they feel the need to forage for food or explore. They are not fussy eaters. Able to adapt to a wide variety of foods, they make the best of whatever is available.

Mice exemplify "safety in numbers." Their colonial lifestyle increases the chances for individual survival. As a result, mice have developed special behaviors and various forms of communication. A mouse must be able to

Mice keep themselves very clean. You will often see your mouse groom itself and its companions. Grooming is so important to good mouse health that lack of grooming is one of the early signs of illness.

recognize and identify other members of its colony and interact with each individual in an appropriate manner.

As you observe your mouse on a daily basis, you will appreciate the fact that almost everything your mouse does, it does for a good reason. Its behavior and communication reflect millions of years of ancestral development, making it possible for the mouse, one of the most adaptable rodent species, to survive to the present day.

Following are some basic mouse behaviors to help you learn how to interpret your mouse's moods and attitudes.

The Basics

Sense of Smell, Scent Marking, and Olfactory Signals

Mice necessarily have an excellent sense of smell to help them identify other animals and

═CHECKLIST═

Communication

Mice communicate in many ways:
1 Sense of smell and olfactory signals
2 Sense of touch, or tactile communication
3 Sense of hearing and vocalization
4 Body language, visual cues

avoid predators. Strange odors, including the scent of an unknown human, can induce stress responses in mice.

A large part of mouse communication is accomplished by sense of smell. Urine is used extensively as a form of communication among mice. Mice mark their territory by leaving drops of urine on objects and areas. Urine deposition is also a means to identify individuals or groups of animals. Mouse urine contains pheromones, chemical signals that can be perceived by other animals. Mice use keen sense of smell to identify their nests and each other, and to determine when the time is right for breeding. Male mice scent-mark more frequently than females.

Mice also have scent glands that secrete pheromones. Pheromones from adult mice play an important role in reproduction and can accelerate or delay the onset of puberty of younger mice in the colony, induce an estrous cycle, synchronize estrous cycles among females, or prevent implantation of embryos (see Raising Mice, page 81).

Sense of Touch, Grooming, and Tactile Communication

Touch: Because they have poor eyesight, mice rely heavily on their sense of touch. They use their whiskers (vibrissae) to help them navigate tunnels and burrows and to make contact with surfaces, walls, and obstacles. They also use their whiskers to identify other mice in the nest. When two mice meet for the first time, and if the encounter is not an aggressive one, they usually begin their introductions by making contact with their whiskers and sniffing each other.

Grooming: Mice are meticulous about their coats and groom themselves frequently. Mice that have established amiable relationships in the colony enjoy grooming one another.

Huddling: Huddling is an important aspect of mouse life, health, safety, and well-being. Mice love to huddle. By huddling together in a nest, mice that coexist peacefully can keep warm and share the same body scents.

Sense of Hearing and Vocalization

Mice make a variety of sounds, although to humans they simply sound like high-pitched squeaks. Mice communicate in the ultrasonic range during sexual encounters. Baby mice call to their parents in the ultrasonic range in the first 16 days of life. During antagonistic encounters, protest squeaks or squeaks of aggression can clearly be heard.

Mice can hear sounds ranging from 80 Hz to 100 kHz. Their hearing is most keen at 15 kHz to 20 kHz and at 50 kHz. Although baby mice cannot hear until they are at least 11 days of age, they can emit distress calls to their parents in the ultrasonic range, beyond human hearing. They can call to their parents without being heard by some predators. This is a remarkable adaptation for survival in the wild.

Body Language

It is easy to tell when your mouse feels comfortable and secure. Its sense of well-being is evident as it explores its surroundings, runs in the exercise wheel, grooms itself and its companions, climbs, digs, forages, and snacks on favorite foods. All of these activities are signs of a happy, healthy mouse.

Curiosity and interest: Mice are very inquisitive animals. New situations always interest them. When your mouse is curious or interested in something, it will rear up, or climb up to the top of the cage, or push its nose as high as possible, sniffing the air. A tame mouse that is used to being handled will climb into your hand if you place it gently in the cage.

Fear: If your mouse is startled or frightened, it will try to run back to its nest box or hiding place immediately. If escape is not possible, it may become aggressive and threatening. It will rear up and press its ears against its head, indicating that it will attempt to fend off the danger and bite. It may also posture itself, ready to take off at a run at the least disturbance. Another mouse tactic is to freeze and remain in place with its ears flattened against its head until it has an opportunity to escape. This defense mechanism works in the wild, where the mouse's brown color serves as a camouflage among the dirt, shrubs, and rocks of its natural environment. If the mouse makes no movement, it has a better chance of avoiding detection by predators.

Mice may be small, but they can become feisty when frightened. If your mouse is startled, allow it time to calm down before you try to pick it up because in its fear it may try to bite you when you handle it.

Unfamiliar territory: Mice have poor eyesight and rely on their vibrissae and sense of smell to find a safe path. Without scent marks to guide it, your mouse will feel uneasy in new surroundings. If it is unsure of its surroundings or is elevated, it will clutch and cling, trying not to fall.

Behaviors and Activities

Sleeping: Mice spend a lot of time sleeping. Although they are basically nocturnal (most active at night), they are also active during the day. Mice exhibit periods of activity and rest throughout the day and night. They tend to sleep for five to ten minutes, wake up, adjust their posture, and drift back to sleep. They particularly enjoy sleeping in communal piles. You may not find your mouse right away if it is sleeping, because mice like to bury themselves in bedding or nesting material and hide while they snooze. Remember that a dozing mouse can be easily startled and wake up in an irritable mood. If your mouse is asleep, make sure that it hears you and has sufficient time to awaken and sniff the air, then approach it slowly and handle it gently.

Nest-building behavior: Mice are avid nest builders. They spend a good deal of time creating the most elaborate nests they can build. One of the ways you can enrich your pet's life

---

TIP

Signs of Stress in Mice
✔ Running in circles
✔ Chewing at bars
✔ Stereotypic, repetitive behavior (such as pacing)
✔ Fur chewing ("barbering")
✔ Convulsing (seizures)

Mice are tiny, but they are eager eaters. Their big appetites can be satisfied with a wide variety of vegetables, fruits, seeds, and grains.

Mice enjoy grooming one another. Grooming is an important social interaction in the colony that helps them to identify each other by scent.

is by providing lots of nesting material for it to shred, arrange, and rearrange. In fact, if mice are not provided with nest-building material, they become extremely stressed and suffer from the deprivation.

Aggressive behavior: Mice that have been raised together as weanlings usually live together peacefully; however, male mice are notorious for their tendency to fight with each other. Males fight to establish dominance or to protect territory or food. This occurs most often when a new mouse is introduced to the colony, or a nonestablished group of mice is housed together. You should always keep male mice that have been used for breeding separated from other male mice, as the

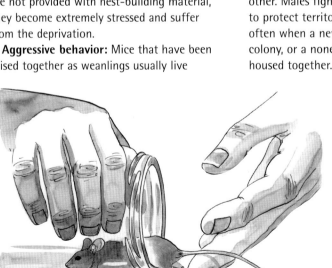

For the inexperienced handler, or for a mouse that is difficult to pick up and acts like it might bite, simply use a can or jar to scoop up the animal. Be sure to cover the jar with one hand so your pet doesn't jump out!

Mice have very poor eyesight and can unknowingly wander into dangerous situations.

Mice are very inquisitive and will investigate every nook and cranny. A large piece of cheese or bread is fun for a mouse to tunnel through and nibble. Just remember to remove it before it spoils!

breeder animals are the most aggressive. Female mice usually get along well together, although fights can occur, particularly among certain strains of mice. (There are more than 200 strains of mice.)

When new animals are added to a stable group, they should be observed to make sure fights and injuries do not occur. Mice can inflict serious bite wounds, targeting the tail, rump, and scrotum of their opponents. Fights can result in the death of one or more mice involved. If the lower-ranking mice are not killed, they will lose weight from stress and the continual attacks that make it difficult to eat and rest. For this reason, you should always provide lots of hiding places and retreats for your mice and never house male mice together. If your mice refuse to be compatible, your only option is to house one mouse per cage. *Fighting animals must always be separated.*

Your mouse has specific inherited behaviors characteristic of its species, including foraging, digging, gnawing, climbing, investigating, playing, and caring for young. Other aspects of its personality will depend on the positive experiences you provide. The more you understand your mouse, the more you will enjoy it.

TIP

Biting

Do not risk being bitten if your animals are fighting. Use a tube or jar to separate and capture the mice. Don't use your hands or fingers!

Once you understand mouse behavior, body language, and activities, you are ready to enjoy handling your pet. Here are some safe ways to pick up your mouse to avoid excessive stress to your pet and minimize your risk of being bitten. Remember to wash your hands thoroughly before and after handling your mice.

The Tail Technique

Mice can safely be picked up by the tail, as long as it is for a brief moment, as in moving the mouse from one cage to another, and is done gently. Simply grasp your mouse by the middle of its tail and lift. Do not lift your mouse by the tip of the tail; your mouse can rapidly spin around and around while it is suspended and the tip of its tail can come off. Also, if you hold your mouse by the tip of its tail, it can swing itself up and over onto your hand or fingers and bite you.

Do not use tweezers or sharp objects to grasp the tail. If you use forceps or tongs to grasp the tail, they should be rubber-cushioned to prevent crushing injury to the tail.

The Jar or Tube Technique

This method is a good one for children who are learning to handle a mouse for the first time. A jar or a tube is slowly lowered into the cage and placed in front of the animal so that it is facing the inside of the container. If your mouse needs some encouragement, simply hold the jar in one hand and use your other hand to gently push its rump forward so it enters the jar. Be sure to cover the top of the jar because your mouse will try to jump out while you are transporting it. If you are using a tube, you will have to cover both ends of the tube until you are ready to release your mouse.

The Two-handed Technique

Use your hands like a scoop to slide underneath the animal and lift it out of the cage. First, stop your mouse's motion by grasping the middle of its tail, then slide one hand under its body and give it support as you lift it. Continue to hold onto your pet's tail to stabilize it until it is safe to let go.

You can also use both hands as a scoop to lift your mouse out of the cage. Be sure to use one hand to support the bottom of your mouse and one hand to cover it so that it cannot jump or fall out of your hands.

The Scruff-of-the-Neck Technique

Many people cringe at the thought of lifting an animal by the skin on the back of its neck, but if done properly, this technique is safe and

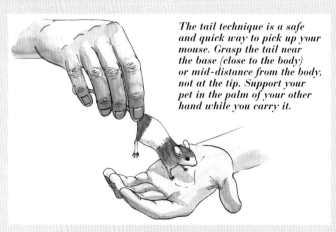

The tail technique is a safe and quick way to pick up your mouse. Grasp the tail near the base (close to the body) or mid-distance from the body, not at the tip. Support your pet in the palm of your other hand while you carry it.

humane for mice. There is a lot of loose skin around the mouse's neck and down its back. The technique requires a bit of practice, but in time you will be able to use this method skillfully. This technique is especially useful for handling mice that are not very tame and may bite. This is the technique your veterinarian is mostly likely to use to examine your mouse or give it an injection or medication.

✔ Approach your mouse calmly and let it know you are there. This way your mouse will not be startled and threaten to bite.

✔ Slowly lower your hand into the cage and grasp your mouse by the middle of its tail, then set it on the cage top or on wire mesh that it can grab with its front feet.

✔ Gently tug on the tail so that the mouse's body stretches out as it clings to the wire mesh with its front feet. With your free hand, grasp the loose skin over the neck, just behind the ears, with your thumb and forefinger.

✔ Now lift the mouse by the scruff of the neck and press its tail into the palm of the same hand so that the fourth and fifth fingers can hold the tail while the thumb and forefinger and middle finger of the same hand hold the mouse.

✔ Make sure you have grasped enough skin so that the mouse cannot turn around in its skin and bite you. Be careful, however, not to grasp the skin too tightly or the mouse will choke. If

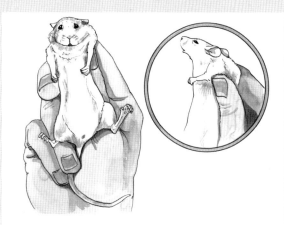

An untamed mouse can be restrained by firmly grasping it by the skin over the neck and back. This method takes some practice but is a safe and humane way to handle unruly mice!

your pet's eyes are bulging noticeably, your grasp is too tight and you should set the animal down and try again.

The Glove Technique

Some people try to use thick gloves when handling mice for the first time. This is unnecessary and cumbersome and sometimes gives a person a false sense of security. Even though mice are small, they can still bite through many kinds of gloves. Because it is difficult to restrain a small animal with thick gloves, there is a tendency to hold on too tightly, squeezing the mouse and making it hard for it to breathe, or crushing it, without even knowing you are harming it. This technique is discouraged.

Warning: *Tweezers and sharp instruments should never be used to grasp mice.*

ACCOMMODATIONS FOR YOUR MOUSE

Mice are common, hardy, resilient rodents. In spite of their many predators in the wild (hawks, owls, skunks, foxes, and cats, to name only a few), mice have been able to survive and reproduce in large numbers in a wide variety of environments worldwide.

Mice are not fussy eaters. Millions of years of evolution have enabled them to adapt to a varied diet, eating whatever is available to ensure survival through the seasons. Seeds and grains are relished as much as fruits and vegetables, and if times are tough, mice can become fierce scavengers, eating whatever they can find to stay alive and reproduce. As you have already surmised, mice are very easy to maintain as pets in captivity. With only minimal effort on your part, you can keep your mouse content and healthy.

Housing your mouse is easy. Depending upon your lifestyle and the amount of time and space you have available, you can design a housing setup that is convenient for you and as complex or simple as you please. Your pet will be per-

An exercise wheel is more than a toy—it is a necessity. It will prevent boredom and help keep your mouse in tip-top shape.

fectly happy in most of the wide variety of cage styles and glass aquaria available from your local pet store.

Housing Considerations

There are five important things to keep in mind when deciding how to house your mouse.
✔ Mice are very social animals and it is recommended that you house at least two mice together. In the wild, mice live in communities and extended family groups, or colonies. If you keep only one mouse, you should set aside a few minutes each day to handle it or provide it with a stimulating activity, such as a maze, toy, or object to investigate. Be sure your mouse always has nesting material available. Nest building is a favorite mouse activity and will keep your pet from becoming bored. A sure way to keep your pet entertained and in good physical condition is to provide it with an exercise running wheel.

If you keep more than one mouse, remember that males will fight and injure or kill each other. Unless you are planning on raising mice, house only female mice together. If you must have a male mouse, house it only with a female and be prepared to find homes for the many offspring they will produce.

✔ Mice can chew their way out of almost anything. Chewing is an important mouse activity. The front teeth (incisors) continually grow throughout life and must be worn down by chewing. For this reason, wood, cardboard, and plastic cages are not suitable for mice.

✔ Mice are excellent climbers and can squeeze through the tiniest openings. Be sure your mouse's cage has a secure door and lid and that the wire mesh or bar spacing of the cage is close enough together to prevent escape.

✔ Mouse urine has a very strong odor. Your pet's home should be easy to clean, nonporous, and resistant to moisture, salts, and cleansers. The cage bedding will need to be changed at least once a week, possibly more often, depending on the number of mice you house in each cage. Be sure to use a secure temporary holding cage to house your mice while you are changing their home cage.

✔ Mice are highly allergenic. This means that over time, you can become allergic to your mice. This is a risk all pet owners take, because prolonged exposure to animal dander, saliva, and urine can cause many people to become allergic to their pets. Mouse urine is especially allergenic, so with this in mind, you should take necessary precautions for yourself and your family to reduce the chances of developing an allergy to your pet mouse. For example, it would be wise to wear a mask, goggles, and gloves (vinyl gloves are recommended because some people are allergic to latex materials) when you change the cage bedding. This may sound like an extreme measure, but it is an effective way to reduce the amount of fine particles of dust that are contaminated with urine and dander from coming into contact with your eyes, nose, mouth, and skin. (Gloves, mask, and goggles are required for personnel involved in cage changing or cleaning in research laboratories, where allergies to mice are not uncommon and are a well-documented personnel health hazard.) Remember to wash your hands thoroughly after changing the bedding or handling your pet.

It is also highly recommended that you place your mouse cage somewhere in the home where there is less chance of prolonged exposure to the cage bedding dust; for example, don't keep your pet's home in your bedroom.

Mice are content in just about any kind of housing, from a simple shoe-box style cage to a more elaborate multitiered cage. Be sure all lids and doors are securely fastened and that the space between bars or grids is small enough to prevent escape.

Nesting Material

Mice are elaborate nest builders, whether they are raising a family or not. Nest building is an important mouse activity and necessary for their well-being. Nesting material should be clean and safe for your mice. Hay, straw, shredded filter paper (a mouse favorite!), tissues, wood chips, and paper towels all make excellent nesting material. Do not use corncob bedding for nesting material because it is too highly absorbent and rapidly dehydrates young mice through the skin surface. Improper bedding material is a common cause of death in newborn mice. Fluffy nesting material from synthetic fabrics or cotton wool is not safe because mice can become caught or tangled in it. You can purchase safe, clean mouse nesting material from your local pet store.

Housing Options

When you think about housing your pet mouse, think about primary and secondary enclosures. The primary enclosure is the actual cage in which your mouse lives. The secondary enclosure is the space that contains

Minimum Cage Size Required

Mice Weight	Floor Space/ Mouse	Minimum Cage Height
<$\frac{1}{3}$ ounce (<10 g)	6 inches^2 (38 cm^2)	5 inches (13 cm)
$\frac{1}{3}$–$\frac{1}{2}$ ounce (10-15 g)	8 inches^2 (50 cm^2)	5 inches (13 cm)
$\frac{1}{2}$–1 ounce (15-28 g)	15 inches^2 (97 cm^2)	8 inches (20 cm)

TIP

Floors

Cages that have solid floors are preferable to those with wire mesh ones. Mice that are housed on grid floors can develop pressure sores on their feet. Male mice can develop urological problems from the wire mesh irritating the genital area. If you use a cage with grid flooring, be sure to provide your mouse with a solid area where it can rest its feet when it desires.

the cage. Your mouse's housing is affected by the conditions in the secondary enclosure (room or area in which the cage is placed) as much as it is affected by the conditions in its home cage. For example, the ventilation, humidity, temperature, lighting, and noise level in the secondary enclosure will affect the comfort of your pet in its primary enclosure, or home cage.

Styles and Sizes

The cage style and size you select will depend upon the number of animals you are housing and the amount of space available in your home.

Plexiglas: A 10-gallon (38-L) Plexiglas aquarium makes a good home because it gives you an excellent view of your small pet and shields it from drafts. A Plexiglas aquarium is also nonporous and can be cleaned and disinfected. It is large enough to comfortably house several mice and provide them with plenty of space for play. There is also enough room for dishes, a water bottle, toys, and an exercise wheel. A tight-fitting, snap-on or clip-on lid is an important

Your pet will make use of any safe hideaway or toy you provide. The type of environment you create is limited only by your imagination. Here a mouse enjoys a miniature rock cave designed for a fish aquarium.

Grass hay makes good bedding material. If you select this option, purchase only clean, safe grass hay that is packaged and marketed specifically for pets.

feature of aquarium housing because, if you have tall toys or branches inside the cage, your pet can easily climb right out the top. The primary disadvantages of a Plexiglas aquarium are its large size, making it cumbersome to clean, and its high walls, which restrict ventilation.

Shoebox: If you want to house your mouse in something smaller, there is a wide variety of mouse cages from which to choose at your local pet store. You may purchase something as simple as a "shoebox" cage. This cage, shaped like a shoebox, measures 8 inches × 12 inches × 5 inches (20 cm × 30 cm × 13 cm), has a wire-rack top to hold a water bottle and food, and can house up to four adult mice. If you decide to buy a wire cage, check that the spacing between the wire mesh or the bars is not more than ½ inch (10 mm). Do not purchase a

wooden cage because it cannot be disinfected and is porous so you cannot eliminate the mouse urine odor from the cage. In any case, your mouse would, in time, chew its way out of a wooden cage and escape. A plastic cage is discouraged unless it is designed in such a way that there is no possible way your mouse can chew on it. If you are using a cage or lid that has a hole cut away for the insertion of a water bottle sipper tube, make sure the hole is not large enough to permit escape.

Multilevel wire cage: For the creative mouse owner, who has the space and enjoys watching busy mice explore, a multilevel wire cage is ideal. This type of caging offers your pet more opportunity to exercise by climbing up and down walls and ramps. Another excellent cage option is a two-tiered wire cage on top of an

The number of mice you keep will determine how often you should clean the cage. Your mice should always have clean, dry bedding.

aquarium, with a wire ramp leading from the aquarium floor up to the wire cage. This provides additional play and exploration space for your pet and allows it to select a warmer, sheltered, draft-free environment, and ventilation, when desired.

Size: Cage size is one of the most important aspects of mouse health. Mice become very stressed if they are overcrowded. Although it may appear that your mice spend most of their time huddled together in the nest, they really do require a good deal of space to play, explore, and seek privacy. The guidelines on page 39 are for minimal space requirements; however, if you can provide your pet with larger accommodations, it is highly recommended.

Cedar and pine shavings look and smell nice, but they contain substances that can cause health problems for mice, including itchy skin. Aspen shavings are recommended for cage bedding.

Cleaning and Conflict

Your mice will need to have their cage cleaned and bedding changed regularly to prevent odors and keep them healthy. High levels of carbon dioxide and ammonia from urine make mice more susceptible to disease and infections. Knowing just when to clean your pet's cage is a bit of a balancing act. On the one hand, you want to keep odors to a minimum for your health and the health of your pets. On the other hand, mice use urine extensively to scent-mark, and when you clean the cage you disturb the scent markings and stress your mice. Stressed mice often become more aggressive and are more likely to fight among themselves. How frequently you clean the cage depends upon the number of mice you keep and the size of the cage. Following are four different acceptable methods for cage cleaning. Try them and see which way works best for you and minimizes disturbance among your mice. Remember, no matter what, your mice should always have dry bedding.

1. Clean the cage and introduce all fresh bedding at the same time. This method works best if you are housing aggressive males. It removes scents so that no one male can immediately claim or fight over territory.

2. Clean the cage and introduce 90 percent fresh bedding, keeping 10 percent of the old bedding that is not soiled. This method is satisfactory when housing breeding animals, in which there is only one male and one or more females.

3. Do not clean the cage, but introduce all new bedding material. This causes the most aggression in males because the top-ranking male is still in his home territory but has no olfactory cues for other males as his scent marks have been removed. It is as if the male himself had been removed, so other males try to scent-mark the territory as their own and battles ensue. This method is appropriate for breeding colonies in which only one male is housed.

4. Remove bedding only from soiled areas of the cage. This method is most appropriate for breeding colonies in which only one male is housed, or when there is a new litter and you do not wish to disturb the mother and babies.

Lighting

Lighting, or illumination or photoperiod, refers to the intensity, spectrum (wavelength), and duration of light exposure. Lighting can be natural (sunlight) or artificial (lightbulbs). Light intensity is usually expressed as footcandles (ftc). Your home is probably illuminated at around 100 ftc, which is a comfortable level for people. Scientists have learned that when mice are exposed to 100 ftc of light at eye level, a degeneration of the retinas of the eyes occurs, called "phototoxic retinopathy." Albino mice are more sensitive than colored mice because they have no pigmentation in their eyes to protect

TIP

Monitor Your Animals

Always monitor your animals for signs of fighting after cleaning the cage.

Do not clean the cage if there is a new litter one week of age or younger.

Neonates become stressed very easily. The mother also may become stressed and cannibalize (eat) her young.

them from light, and young mice are more sensitive than adult mice. Researchers have determined that ideally, mice should not be exposed to more than 25 ftc of light and that the light should be diffuse.

Remember that the light level in your pet's cage is more important than the light level in the room. Mice that are housed in solid-walled cages, such as opaque shoebox-type cages or steel cages, are not exposed to as much light as mice that are housed in clear plastic cages or Plexiglas aquaria.

Hiding places: Wild mice avoid eye injury caused by bright light because they spend their daylight hours sleeping in dim hideaways. You can give your mouse ways to modify its own light exposure by providing it with hiding places, tunnels, and barriers. Under these conditions, your mouse will probably be exposed to only 10 to 50 ftc of light and it is unlikely that its eyes will be damaged by the lighting in your home. Whenever possible, place your pet's cage in an area with subdued light. You can also make use of various bafflings and barriers to block out bright light and make the cage more interesting, private, and secure.

Ideal lighting: Although your pet's eyes are sensitive to bright light, in many cases any damage to its eyes caused by exposure to bright light can be reversed over time if the animal is returned to subdued lighting. An ideal lighting system for a mouse breeding colony would be 10 hours of light during the day and 14 hours of dark at night. They also do well with 12 hours of light and 12 hours of darkness; however, you do not have to follow such a strict schedule if it is not convenient for you. Mice have been known to change their activity schedules to correspond to that of the light cycles. If you

do not work conventional hours, your mouse will adapt and still be awake to provide hours of entertainment for you when you return home. Mice are very adaptable. The main thing is to make sure your mice are not exposed to bright light that can damage their eyes.

Red light: Mice are insensitive to red light, so if you would like to use red light to observe your pets' nighttime activities, you can do this safely without damaging their eyes.

Lighting plays an important role in your pet's physiology and hormone levels. If you are planning on raising mice, keep in mind that the duration of light exposure, but not its intensity, plays a key role in the reproductive cycle of the mouse (see Raising Mice, page 81).

Temperature, Humidity, and Ventilation

Good ventilation is important to maintain temperature and humidity at comfortable levels in your pet's primary and secondary enclosures. The temperature and humidity in the room may vary significantly from the temperature and humidity in your mouse's cage. For example, if your pet is housed in a Plexiglas aquarium that is placed in direct sunlight, the cage can be intolerably hot while the room remains at a comfortable temperature. Remember that mice are extremely sensitive to heat and will die when the temperature reaches 98.6°F (37°C). If temperature changes are sudden, your mice can begin to die when the temperature reaches 78°F (25.5°C). Place your pet's cage in an area where there is good ventilation but where it cannot become overheated or exposed to drafts.

Although mice can tolerate temperatures between 65 and 79°F (18 to 26°C) if there is

good ventilation, housing at room temperature (69 to 72°F [21 to 22.2°C]) is recommended because mice have a relatively low tolerance to heat compared to some other animals. Humidity should be between 40 and 70 percent, and preferably around 50 to 55 percent. Remember that it will probably be more humid inside your mouse's cage, particularly if the cage walls are solid, than outside the cage.

Temperature and Humidity

Mice are comfortable at room temperature (69 to 72°F [21 to 22.2°C]). Mice should be protected from drafts, temperature variations, heat, cold, and excessive dryness. Humidity should be 50 to 55 percent to avoid dehydration, skin problems, and other possible medical problems, such as ringtail. This is especially important for baby mice. Exchange of fresh air is also important. Mice require well-ventilated, but not

Mice are excellent climbers. They are also expert escape artists, so make sure the cage is always securely fastened!

drafty, enclosures. They should not be placed near heaters, radiators, or fans, or in areas of direct sunlight. This is especially critical for mice housed in glass aquaria where exposure to direct sunlight can elevate temperatures beyond the comfort and safety zone (greenhouse effect). When temperatures reach 98.6°F (37°C), mice quickly succumb to heatstroke and die.

Noise

High-pitched sounds, such as clanging metal, telephones, alarms, doorbells, faucets, computers, and cleaning noises can be very stressful to mice. In fact, in some mice, high-pitched sounds can cause them to have a seizure or other health-

Creative mice will find more than one way to use an exercise wheel!

Be sure to give your mice safe hiding places. Hideaways provide privacy and protect your pets' sensitive eyes from the light.

A mouse will clean and groom itself thoroughly from its nose to its toes.

TIP

Screens

To help eliminate stressful noises, place a screen of thick rubber or Styrofoam around the outside of the cage to absorb the sound. The screen will also help reduce the light intensity.

related problems. Mice can become very sensitized to loud noises. Loud noises interfere with communication between mother mice and the babies, or between adult mice. Exposure to loud noises can also cause some individuals to convulse later in life. Loud noises have been shown to cause toxicity in pregnant mice and their unborn young (embryotoxicity). This doesn't mean that you have to tiptoe around the house when you are in the presence of your pet. In fact, many of the sounds that we can hear are inaudible to rodents. For example, humans hear in the 1 to 4 kilocycle range, whereas rodents hear best at 10 to 40 kilocycles. Just remember that some noises, depending upon their frequency and intensity, can be stressful or frightening to your mouse. You can eliminate this stress for your pet by finding a place to keep its cage where there is peace and quiet.

Note: Some people have suggested playing soft background music to reduce stress in mice subjected to loud noises, but whether this has any benefit remains to be determined.

Toxicity

Mice are very sensitive to certain chemical compounds. Products that contain essential oils such as menthol or eucalyptol, found in disinfectants and air fresheners, can make your pet very ill. In addition, insecticides (ant and roach sprays) can kill your mouse. Be sure to keep its housing isolated from areas where any of these products might be used in your home.

Exercise

Mice are very active animals that love to run. An exercise wheel is an excellent form of entertainment for your pet and helps keep it healthy and in good physical condition. Your mouse will use its running wheel every day, without fail.

There are several sizes and models of exercise wheels. An exercise wheel with a solid floor is recommended because this style of running wheel is safer than a wheel with rungs and the mouse's tail cannot be pinched in one of the wheel supports. Also, a solid floor is more comfortable for tiny feet. This is especially important for an animal that runs as much as mice do!

Wheels can be free-standing or attached to the cage wall. Before you buy an exercise wheel, decide which model will be most suitable for your mouse's home. For example, a free-standing wire wheel takes up floor space that could be better used as a play area. More important, a free-standing wheel can be a potential danger if one mouse is running in it and another mouse tries to jump on while the wheel is in motion. It is possible for the second animal to become trapped between the support that runs the diameter of the wheel and the vertical bar of the wheel stand. Wheels that attach to the side of the cage and have a solid floor and wall are safest, but many of these are made of plastic. You will probably have to replace them periodically because your mouse can chew and destroy them.

An exercise wheel is such a popular mouse toy that you might want to consider purchasing two wheels if you are housing several mice together and there is enough space in the cage.

There are other items you can make or purchase to enhance your pet's enjoyment and encourage exercise. These include platforms, tubes, ladders, ramps, barriers, mazes, and branches to climb.

Grooming

You will notice that your mouse keeps itself meticulously clean; in fact, if your mouse does not keep itself clean and groomed, it is a sign of poor health. So don't worry about bathing or grooming your pet. There is no need to purchase any tiny combs, brushes, or shampoos for it. Actually, a water bath could cause a mouse to become chilled and sick. Shampoo products could also make your mouse ill. Never use any shampoos or products containing pesticides to kill parasites on the skin. These products are manufactured with larger animals, such as dogs or cats, in mind. The dose of active chemicals in these products could kill your mouse. Even shampoos that do not contain pesticides can be harmful. Besides, shampoos and perfumed grooming products will interfere with the mouse's natural odors, which play an important role in the mouse's social life with regard to behavior, breeding, territoriality, and community activities in the colony.

If you think your mouse has a skin condition that needs attention, or that it may have parasites in its fur, contact your veterinarian. It is important to know exactly what the problem is. Your veterinarian can tell you if the problem is contagious to your other mice, your other pets, or you. If treatment is required, your veterinarian will know which product to use and how much is safe to use on such a tiny animal. This is very important, because, as previously discussed, many products are toxic to mice.

Bottles and Dishes

Water Bottles

Fresh water should be available at all times, provided in a water bottle with a sipper tube. Water dishes are not practical for mice because the water can easily become soiled and contaminated, or spill and dampen the cage bedding. A water bottle holds more water than a dish, reducing the risk that your pet will run out of water during the day or in the event you are absent from home longer than anticipated. It can be fastened to the outside of the cage, leaving more cage space available for a play area. And, if your mouse has not used a water bottle before, its keen sense of smell will direct it to the water source. It will learn to use the bottle's sipper tube immediately.

Water bottles also have disadvantages that are important to consider in relation to your mouse's health. The sipper tubes can become plugged, making it impossible for your mouse to obtain water. Bacteria can grow and multiply in dirty sipper tubes and contaminate the water, causing illness (see Feeding Your Mouse, page 57).

Feeders

Food should be provided in feeders that attach to the wall of the cage, or in dishes that are chew-proof and heavy enough that they cannot be tipped, such as a ceramic bowl.

Top left: Make sure your mouse has plenty of fresh water available at all times.
Top right: Mice will eat out of a dish, but they usually take extra food to hide under the bedding. Use a chew-proof, sturdy dish that doesn't tip.
Bottom left: Mice enjoy grooming each other, even when it interferes with mealtime!

Water bottles and food dishes should be cleaned and refilled daily. Sipper tubes should be checked daily to be sure they are working properly and cleaned thoroughly each day with a round brush.

Toys for Mice

Mice are very playful animals. They are active year-round and do not hibernate. When housed together they spend much of their recreation time simply interacting with each other. Because of their active and curious nature, you will not only want to keep your mice in a cage large enough for them to play and socialize, but you

Using a food dish makes it easier for you to monitor your pet's food intake and food preferences; however, even if your mouse's food dish is empty, there will probably be at least one pile of food hidden under the bedding. Some cages are equipped with lids that hold water bottles and food. If you use this type of housing, you will have to feed rodent blocks because smaller-sized foods will fall through the grates.

will also want to give them plenty of safe and interesting toys. Toys are a worthwhile investment in your pets' overall well-being, providing additional stimulus for exploration and play. You will enjoy observing firsthand their interesting play behavior.

There is a wide variety of rodent toys available from your local pet store, including chew sticks, nest boxes, hideaway houses, ladders, ramps, and tunnel tubes.

Chew Toys

Mice love to chew and because their front teeth grow continually and must be worn down, they need a constant supply of safe rodent chew toys, such as wooden sticks. It is best to purchase safe rodent chew sticks from a pet store but if you decide to provide your mice with twigs and sticks, be certain that these materials do not come from any poisonous or potentially harmful plant or tree. Aspen wood makes excellent rodent chew sticks.

Playhouses and Nest Boxes

Your mice will enjoy any type of playhouse, nest box, or hideaway house that you provide. Once again, remember that whatever toys you select, your mouse will chew on them, so be sure they are made of nontoxic materials.

You may buy tunnel tubes from your local pet store or you can make them yourself from PVC pipe material. PVC is safe for your pet, inexpensive, and can be easily cleaned and reused. Do not use cardboard tubing from paper towel rolls,

If the exercise wheel gets too crowded, consider putting another wheel in the cage.

Mice can run fast and climb high. Be sure your mouse's cage top is securely fastened to prevent escape.

as it can wriggle its way out between your fingers and slip away or fall. Once your mouse is loose, it faces countless life-threatening situations in your cozy home.

Capturing a runaway mouse can be extremely difficult and take some time. Just in case your mouse escapes, you need to know what potential household hazards it may encounter so you can correct the situation in advance.

toilet paper rolls, or gift-wrapping paper rolls. Most of these tubes (98 to 99 percent) are made from recycled materials and may contain ink residues or other contaminants. Also, it is possible that some of the glues used to make the cardboard tubes may contain toxins.

Mice are very easy to please and will find creative ways to entertain you with almost any safe toy you offer.

Household Hazards

Some of the more fun aspects of mice—their inquisitive nature, tiny size, activity level, and speed—also create some of the biggest problems for their safety. Because they are so small, they are able to fit through spaces you would never think possible. If they can squeeze their head through any crack, the rest of the body follows easily. And because they are so quick, they are excellent escape artists. For these reasons it is impossible to keep a mouse in a wooden or cardboard container, even temporarily, because it will chew its way out in no time. Even holding a mouse can be a challenge,

Sticky Traps, Snap Traps, and Rodent Poisons

Go through your house and look for any spaces or holes that your mouse can crawl into, as well as anything it can fall into where it can be trapped. And speaking of traps, if you have any sticky or snap traps set in your house or garage, pick them up immediately. Also be sure to pick up any rodent bait or poison that may have been left out for wild vermin. They are as deadly for your domestic pet as they are for wild rodents.

Household Chemicals

Mice can hide in cabinets where there are often household products such as cleaning agents, bug sprays, paints, fertilizers, pesticide baits, and other poisonous chemicals. All of these substances are extremely dangerous and potentially deadly for your pet if it comes in contact with them. Some types of paints can be toxic to your mouse if it chews on wooden baseboards or walls.

Electrical Shock

Unplug and remove any electrical cords that may be within your escaped mouse's reach. Electrocution from gnawing on an electrical cord is a real potential danger that would cost your pet its life and possibly cause an electrical fire.

Appliances

Before you do the laundry, check your clothing, especially the pockets. A laundry basket makes a warm hiding place. Sadly, more than one pocket pet has been found, too late, inside the washer or dryer.

Be very careful when you vacuum under and behind furniture—an unsuspecting mouse can easily be sucked up the vacuum hose. As surprising as it sounds, it is not an unusual pocket pet accident!

Other Pets

If you have other pets in the house, remember that they pose a serious threat to your mouse. A gentle dog or curious cat quickly regains its instincts to hunt or kill small prey, especially when stimulated by the sight of a small animal trying to flee. A fatal accident can take place in a split second. There will also be less chance of your mouse coming out of its hiding place if it hears and smells other animals in the area. Until your mouse is recovered, put your other pets in a secure place where they cannot hurt it when it does finally come out of hiding.

If there are small children in the house, ask their assistance in finding the mouse. Children are very eager to be helpful and are remarkably skilled at finding the smallest of things,

An escaped mouse can be hide in almost any small, dark place.

but remind the child not to try to grab the animal when it is found. In the excitement a small mouse can easily be squeezed too tightly, stepped on, or accidentally crushed or injured. A startled mouse will bite, too. A small child may inadvertently frighten your pet away before you arrive and capture it, so be sure you give good instructions to everyone involved in the capture program before you begin!

Outside Doors

Make sure all doors to the outside or the garage are closed. If your mouse escapes to the garage, it will be exposed to additional hazards and poisons. For example, your mouse might find a few drops of antifreeze (ethylene glycol) on the garage floor. Antifreeze has a sweet taste that appeals to animals, but is a deadly poison that causes kidney failure in a very short time. If your mouse escapes to the outdoors, it will be virtually impossible to find it and it will certainly not survive the dangers of automobiles, neighborhood animals, wild birds, and harsh weather conditions. It will also be susceptible to contracting diseases spread by wild rodents.

Crushing Injuries

Everyone in the house must pay close attention to where they step. Your mouse can dart out from under an object and be underfoot before you know it. Mice also like to hide in dark places, so inspect your closets and check the insides of your shoes before you put them on. As strange as it sounds, being accidentally crushed inside a shoe is not an unusual mouse accident. Check the furniture before you sit down on it. Your mouse could be hiding under the cushions of a couch or chair.

Toilets

Be sure to keep the seat and lid down on the toilet. Mice are good climbers and if there are any objects near the toilet that your mouse can climb up on, such as a clothes hamper or wicker basket, it is possible for your pet to fall inside the toilet bowl. Once inside, your mouse cannot escape and will become chilled and quickly

Fresh food and water, a playhouse, and friends: the perfect setting for a happy mouse.

drown. Toilet drownings are common pocket pet accidents, so don't let your mouse become one of the statistics!

Capturing Your Mouse

If your mouse escapes, but is very tame, you might be able to capture it by setting its cage or nest box on the floor. Leave an opening to the cage or nest box and bait it with your pet's favorite treat, then leave the area. It helps to turn down the lights and be very quiet. This helps your mouse to calm down after the excitement of its escape and free run of the house. If your pet is tired and hungry, and you are very lucky, it may return to its home to eat and rest.

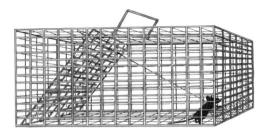

It may be necessary to buy or rent a humane trap in order to catch your escaped pet.

If you mouse doesn't come home on its own, you will have to actively look for it before it gets into trouble. Be prepared to capture your mouse when you do find it. A tightly woven butterfly net with a long handle is sometimes useful, but you must be careful not to inadvertently hit your mouse with the hard edge of the net framework. You can also try using a small hand towel as a net to throw over your pet. Once the cloth is over the animal, you must act quickly to roll the mouse up in the material and transfer it to its cage. You can also try using a box to place over your mouse, but this can be cumbersome and you might accidentally injure your pet in the process.

A good option is to purchase a small humane trap, such as a Hav-A-Hart trap for mice, at the local pet shop or feed store. If you cannot purchase a trap, you may be able to rent or borrow one from your local animal shelter or veterinarian. Bait the trap with your mouse's favorite treat—raisins, apples, peanuts, and sunflower seeds are very popular—and place it in an easily accessible and quiet area.

If you are using a trap, you are most likely to catch your mouse during the evening hours when it is most active. It will probably be hidden and sleeping during the day.

CHECKLIST

Making a Safe and Inexpensive Homemade Trap

1 Simply place a treat in a large coffee can or a small bucket.

2 Tilt the can or bucket against a small ramp. The ramp can be made of a box, board, or mesh material.

3 Tilt the ramp in such a way that when your mouse climbs to the top of the ramp, it will also be at the top of the container. Following its sense of smell, and unable to distinguish the trap with its poor eyesight, your mouse will slide in after the bait but will not be able to climb up the smooth sides of the can or bucket.

Whatever kind of traps you use, be sure to check them several times a day. By the time you catch your mouse it may be very hungry and thirsty and may need immediate care.

A tiny mouse cannot defend itself against other household pets. This little mouse better "let sleeping dogs lie."

Recommended Cage Features

One of the most important things to do when you are selecting a cage for your pet is to choose one that is non-porous and easy to clean and disinfect. You should also select a cage style that provides you a good view of your pet, so you can watch its activities.

✔ The cage should be made of glass, Plexiglas, or stainless steel. A standard 10-gallon (38-L) glass aquarium, with an escape-proof screen or wire-mesh lid, makes a good cage.

✔ Select a cage that allows you easy access to your pet, with ample space to reach in and catch it. If your cage is tall, or multitiered, and has only one opening, it is more convenient if the door is located on the front of the cage, rather than the top.

✔ Mice also do well in shoe-box-shaped cages with snap-on stainless steel tops that hold rodent blocks and water bottles. If you use this type of cage, be sure that the sipper tube of the water bottle is long enough for your mice to reach. Baby mice have trouble reaching sipper tubes so you may have to purchase an extra-long sipper tube for them. Be sure that the hole for the sipper tube is not so large that your mice can crawl out through it and escape.

✔ Mice are more comfortable living directly on bedding, as opposed to being elevated above the floor pan and housed directly on a wire floor.

✔ Try to avoid purchasing a cage that prevents you from housing your mice directly on bedding material.

✔ If you must house your mice on wire temporarily until you can purchase a better cage, make sure the floor mesh spacing is large enough to allow waste material to drop through to the floor pan, but small enough to prevent your pets' feet from getting caught or injured in between the wire mesh, and give your mice a footrest area by providing them with a flat piece of pinewood.

✔ If your mice do not have a solid surface on which to rest their feet, they can develop sores from the continual pressure of the wire-mesh floor against their feet or urological problems from constant wire contact against their genitals.

✔ Be sure that the wood you place in the cage has not been chemically treated or preserved, as is done for wooden boards used in construction. Chemicals and preservatives can be toxic to your pets.

✔ The board should also be free of staples, nails, and any other foreign object that can cause injury or be chewed or swallowed. Of course, you will have to periodically replace the wooden footrest because your mice will eventually chew it up!

Select a cage style that lets you observe your pet's activities. You can create simple hideaways and accessories from nontoxic wooden or cardboard boxes, PVC tubes, sticks, and nonpoisonous branches.

Mice are good climbers so it is important to house them in a well-enclosed cage with a secure, latching door or lid.

Bedding Material

Bedding material is one of the most important aspects affecting your pet's health. Your pet will soil only one or two areas of its cage and keep the rest of the cage clean for food storage and nesting.

✔ A 2-inch (5-cm) depth of bedding material is sufficient coverage for the cage floor.

✔ A semiabsorbent material should be used to prevent urine contact with the skin.

✔ Wood shavings or chips, cellulose-based chips, and shredded filter paper are all excellent bedding material.

✔ If you use wood shavings, aspen shavings are recommended. Although pine and cedar shavings may smell nice and look pretty, the aromatic substances they contain to mask odors also cause physiological changes and can cause itchy skin, liver problems, or other health problems. Only shavings that are packaged and indicated for direct-contact use as bedding material for caged pets should be used in your mouse's cage.

✔ Shavings that are sold for horse stalls or stored in open outdoor bins may be contaminated with undesirable material or even urine and germs from wild rodents. These shavings can pose a health risk for your pet and possibly contain rodent disease organisms. Shavings absorb urine and odors and should be changed at least once a week. If several animals are housed together the shavings may need to be replaced twice a week or more often as necessary.

✔ If you use corncob bedding, check it carefully to make sure it is not moldy; it may contain toxins called mycotoxins. Corncob bedding can cause dehydration and death in very young

An exercise wheel that attaches to the cage wall and has a solid floor is safer for mice and more comfortable for their tiny feet.

mice and is not recommended for breeding colonies and newborns.

✔ Do not use shredded newspaper for bedding; this material allows too much moisture to remain in contact with the animals and may contain ink toxins.

✔ Be sure that the bedding material you use is as dust-free as possible. Bedding that contains a lot of dust and fine particles can be very irritating to your mouse's lungs and cause wheezing, sneezing, and other respiratory problems.

Houses

Mice build their nests in the cage bedding, but they still enjoy having a little house in which to hide. Every cage should contain at least one nest box to provide a quiet hiding place. You can make inexpensive houses out of clean milk cartons, which give your mouse the darkness, warmth, and quiet it would experience in an underground burrow. If your mouse has babies and decides to move them to the nest box, whenever you need to check on them you can lift the carton just enough to take a peek. Your mouse will eventually chew the milk carton to pieces but that's all right; they are easy to replace!

Mice are omnivorous. They will eat whatever seeds, fruits, and grains they can find. Because mice are not fussy eaters, and because their nutritional requirements are well known, providing a balanced, nutritious diet for your mouse is extremely easy.

What to Feed

Proper nutrition plays an important role in your pet's overall health, life span, and reproduction. The majority of the diet should consist of a balanced, high-quality commercial mouse chow consisting of at least 20 percent protein. Be sure the food you provide is fresh and check daily to be certain any food your mouse has hidden and stashed is free of mold. Store all food in closed containers in a cool, dry place.

Commercial Rodent Food

Mice thrive on the large selection of commercial mouse chow available from pet stores. Most of your mouse's diet should consist of commercial mouse chow provided free choice (also called free feeding, or *ad libidum*), which means around-the-clock food availability. Mice enjoy rodent blocks, a balanced rodent diet manufactured into small, hard blocks. They are nutritious and help wear down the teeth.

Freshness: Be sure the food you provide is fresh. To ensure the freshness of the mouse

A baby mouse samples some solid food.

chow you purchase, check the milling date on the food package to verify the shelf life of the product. If the food is old, the vitamins in the food will lose their potency and no longer be effective. Standard laboratory recommendations are to feed chow that is no older than six months (180 days) from the time of milling. You should discard any food that is more than 180 days old because once the food package has been opened and the food has been exposed to atmospheric conditions, vitamins begin to lose their potency.

Treats

Your mouse will enjoy various treats of seeds and grains, which should be raw and unsalted. Mice also enjoy treats available from your pet store. Well-washed raw fruits, vegetables, grains, and nuts are a good source of nutrition. When you feed your mice fruits and vegetables, be sure to remove them from the cage before they spoil.

Whatever you feed your mouse, make sure a quality commercial mouse chow makes up the majority of the diet and limit treats to a

Vitamins

Mice can synthesize their own vitamin C and efficiently recover many B vitamins through the practice of coprophagy (eating their own feces). If you feed your mouse a well-balanced, nutritional commercial mouse chow, there should be no need for you to supplement your pet's diet with vitamins.

reasonable amount. Avoid feeding too many treats, especially those high in sugar content. If your mouse consumes too many treats, it will eat less of its mouse chow and will not receive a balanced diet. It will also be more prone to nutritional disorders and medical problems such as obesity. For example, too many fruits and vegetables could cause intestinal upset and diarrhea.

Mice will consume about ½ ounce (15 g) of food and ½ ounce (15 ml) of water per 3½ ounces (100 g) of body weight daily. They will consume most of their food at night, although they will eat periodically around the clock. Their forepaws are used to grab large pieces of food that they chip into smaller particles with their strong incisors and then grind with their molars.

If your mice have babies, they will appreciate small pieces of fruit to provide moisture, especially if the babies cannot yet reach the sipper tubes.

A combination of fresh mouse chow, seeds, nuts, grains, and raw fruits and vegetables makes mealtime interesting and nutritious and will help keep your mouse healthy.

Note: Corn has been known to cause itchy, dry skin and scratching in some animals so if your mouse experiences any of these symptoms, you may want to remove any corn from its diet.

How Much and How Often

Mice are eager eaters. They should have fresh food and water available at all times. Mice burn up a lot of calories with all their activities and their high metabolic rate. They require even more food if they are growing, pregnant, or nursing their young. Mice will stockpile food in their nest box for safekeeping. It is all right for them to hide away a little bit of food, but if you find a huge stash in the nest box, then it is time to reduce the amount you are feeding. Be sure to remove any food in the cache before it spoils or becomes moldy.

If your mice have babies, it is safer to have a little bit of extra food available within their reach. The mother mouse will also need her share of additional food to enable her to provide enough body heat and milk to successfully raise her young.

Potentially Harmful Foods

Do not feed your mice cooked or processed foods. These are not good for them and may be lacking in vitamins or contain food additives and preservatives. Do not feed your mice chocolate, which contains theobromine, a product similar to caffeine, or other candies. If you are not sure about the safety or nutritional benefit of any food type, simply do not feed it to your pet. If you wish to provide a special "treat" other than fresh vegetables, fruits, or seeds, be sure to purchase commercial products from the pet store that are made especially for rodents.

Nutritional Disorders

Rodent nutritional requirements have been studied extensively and are available from publications of the National Academy of Sciences and various feed companies. If your mouse does not receive proper nutrition or a nutritionally balanced diet, it can suffer from a variety of health problems, including diabetes, weight loss, or obesity.

Water

Depending upon where you live, contents of city or well water may vary and could contain additives such as chlorine and chloramine, or high levels of undesirable elements, such as arsenic, or low levels of bacteria. The best water you can provide your pet is the same drinking water you filter or buy for yourself. Do not give your pet distilled, demineralized, or deionized water. Just like humans, animals require natural minerals found in spring water. Commercial

Always check to be sure the sipper tube on the water bottle is not leaking or plugged with bedding material and is low enough for the babies to reach.

bottled drinking water is an inexpensive and safe way to ensure the health of your pet.

Be aware of the following:

✔ Mice should have access to pure, clean drinking water at all times. Water is especially important because most of your pet's diet is dry (pellets, seeds, rodent blocks), and a dry diet increases the need for water. Your mouse will readily drink from a sipper tube.

✔ Water consumption depends on your pet's health, condition, and age. It is also greatly influenced by its activity level and reproductive cycle. If your mouse is pregnant or nursing babies, it may drink more than twice the amount of water it usually does. Room temperature and humidity also affect how much water your mouse consumes. Animals housed

Commercial rodent blocks are nutritious and help keep the teeth properly worn down.

If the weather is warm, or humidity is low, your pet will be thirstier than usual. Always provide more water than your mouse can drink, especially if you are housing several mice together.

As a safety precaution, consider adding an extra water bottle to the cage.

Corn is a favorite of mice, but if your mouse is among the few individuals that are allergic to corn, discontinue feeding it.

This is a good spot to oversee the babies' activities!

Transparent playhouses make it possible for you to watch your pets at play.

in a warm, dry room will drink more than those in cooler, more humid environments.

✔ Always provide more water than your mouse normally drinks. If you are housing several animals together, be sure the water supply is sufficient to provide the animals all the water they will need, plus a little extra.

✔ Check the sipper tube daily to be certain it is functioning properly and is not plugged. Mice are notorious for pushing bedding material up sipper tubes! Many animal deaths have been due to sipper tubes that were plugged

TIP

Water

✔ Give your mouse fresh water every day.

✔ As a safety precaution to prevent bacterial growth and reduce water contamination, you should chlorinate your pet's water. Most research laboratories that house mice and other rodents use the following formula to obtain chlorination at 10 to 12 parts per million:

1 ml (5 drops) of 5.25 percent sodium hypochlorite solution (Clorox) in 5 liters of water

Unless you have many mice and several water bottles to fill, you will not need 5 liters (almost 5 quarts) of water, so another way to chlorinate the water is:

Add one drop of Clorox to one quart or one liter of water, mix well, fill your mouse's water bottle or dish and discard the rest of the water.

✔ Keep an extra water bottle and sipper tube on hand so you will always have a clean set ready to alternate each day.

with bedding material or debris, denying water access to a thirsty pet.

✔ Mice can become ill from contaminated water. Keep your pet's water bottles and sipper tubes meticulously clean and provide fresh water daily.

Baby Mice and Water

If you have baby mice 14 days of age or older, they should also have access to a source of moisture. Although they are not weaned from their mother's milk until they are three to four weeks of age, and should not be separated from their mother before four weeks of age, they must learn how to use a sipper tube or water bottle early in life. Your baby mice will start investigating water sources at about two to three weeks of age. At that time you can provide a small amount of fresh, raw, moist carrot, lettuce, or apple. (Potato is sometimes used as a moisture source for young rodents; however, your baby mice would prefer something less starchy and tastier, such as sweet potato, yam, or jicama. If you do give your mice raw potato, be sure any green parts and the "potato eyes" are removed, as these contain a poison called solanine.) At the end of the day, remember to check your pet's food storage areas and discard old vegetables or fruit so they do not rot or soil the cage.

You should also lower the water bottle so that the sipper tube is 1 to 2 inches (2.5–5 cm) above the cage floor, within reach of the baby mice. Make sure the sipper tube is functioning and is not air-locked. It should not be so low that it comes in contact with the cage bedding. If this happens, the sipper tube can either become plugged or the water may completely wick out into the bedding material. Even worse, a plugged sipper tube is an invitation for bacterial growth and water contamination.

Cleaning the Water Bottle and Sipper Tube

To prevent water contamination, the water bottle should be thoroughly cleaned, rinsed well, and refilled daily. Pay particular attention to the cleanliness of the sipper tube. Bacteria rapidly multiply in sipper tubes, especially when they are plugged with small particles and contaminants. Clean your mouse's dishes and bottles with a mild detergent, like the one you use for your own dishes. Rinse them thoroughly to completely remove all traces of the detergent. You can also soak the bottle and sipper tube for a few minutes in mildly chlorinated water, then rinse them thoroughly several times. If you prefer, you can use boiling water to rinse the water bottle and soak the sipper tube. When the water bottle and sipper tube are rinsed well, and *completely cooled*, fill the water bottle with commercial bottled drinking water sold for human consumption.

CHECKLIST

Feeding

Mice will eat seeds, fruits, and grains. With well-known nutritional requirements, providing a healthy, nutritious, and balanced diet for your mouse is very easy.

1 The majority of your mouse's diet should consist of a balanced, high-quality commercial mouse chow consisting of at least 20 percent protein.

2 There is a large selection of commercial mouse chow and rodent food available at pet supply stores and pet shops. Mice also enjoy rodent blocks, which are balanced rodent diets manufactured into small, hard blocks that help to wear down the teeth.

3 When feeding commercial mouse chow, be sure that the food is fresh. Check the milling date on the package. You should not feed your mouse any chow that was manufactured more than 180 days prior to the date of purchase. Vitamins in old food lose their potency and are no longer effective.

4 Mice also enjoy treats of seeds, well-washed fruits and vegetables, nuts, and grains, which should be served raw and unsalted. When serving your mouse fruits and vegetables, make sure you remove any uneaten treats from the cage before they spoil.

5 Mice should have fresh food and water available at all times. They will consume about ½ ounce (15 g) of food and ½ ounce (15 ml) of water per 3½ ounces (100 g) of body weight daily. Although they will eat periodically around the clock, mice will consume most of their food at night. Commercial bottled drinking water is an inexpensive and safe way to ensure the health of your pet.

HEALTH

The most important health care you can provide your mouse is preventive health care. Preventing problems is much easier than treating problems. Mice are very hardy animals, but if your pet becomes ill, it will need immediate attention. Without a diagnosis and appropriate preventive care, your entire mouse colony can become sick and die.

Signs of a Sick Mouse

Sometimes even the best-cared-for animals become ill. Successful recovery depends upon the type of illness and how early the illness was noticed and treated. To recognize a sick mouse, you must first know how a healthy mouse looks and acts. If your pet is acting sluggish, has a dull coat and looks ruffled, is hunched up in an abnormal posture, or is not eating or drinking, then there is most certainly a problem. The sooner you have the problem diagnosed and begin treatment, the better your pet's chances of recovery.

See page 66 to tell if your mouse is healthy or sick.

If Your Mouse Is Sick

1. The first thing you should do, the moment you notice your pet is ill, is separate it from any other pets you have. This way, if the prob-

The health of your mice, and their newborn babies (bottom right), depends entirely on the quality of care they receive from you.

lem is contagious, you have reduced the chances of spreading disease to your other animals.

2. Isolating your sick mouse gives it a chance to begin its recuperation in peace and quiet without distraction and stress.

3. Place your mouse in a comfortable, dark, quiet place.

4. Continue to keep a close watch on your other mice and separate out any others that may also become ill.

5. Thoroughly wash all housing, toys, dishes, and bottles that were in contact with your sick pet. Discard old food and used bedding and nesting material.

6. Thoroughly wash your hands after handling any sick animal and before handling other pets or food. This will help prevent the possible spread of contagious disease.

7. Contact your veterinarian for advice. An examination is important to diagnose the problem. It is the only way to know exactly what the problem is and if it is contagious to you or your other pets. A prescription medication may be indicated to ensure your pet's survival. Mice are resistant to some medications,

Ways to Tell If Your Mouse Is Healthy

	Healthy Mouse	Sick Mouse
Appearance	Bright, clear eyes. Well-groomed, shiny coat. Robust, good condition.	Dull expression, eyes partially closed. Ruffled coat in poor condition. Thin, losing weight.
Behavior	Alert, active, very sociable. Good appetite. Sits, stands, climbs, runs in exercise wheel, explores and plays.	Lethargic, depressed, slow, irritable. Will not eat or drink. Hunched-up position, inactive.

and sensitive to others, so your veterinarian's expertise is necessary. Since handling and transportation can further upset your sick pet, your veterinarian may make a house call. If you must transport your mouse, it is less stressful if the mouse can travel in its cage. Cover the cage with a large towel to reduce sounds and light that might startle your small companion.

Helping Your Veterinarian Help You

Make a list of all the questions you want to ask your veterinarian. Your veterinarian will also ask you some questions to help make a diagnosis and determine an appropriate treatment. Don't worry if you don't have all the answers; every piece of information will be helpful for your pet.

Before your appointment, make a list of the following information:

✔ How old is your mouse?
✔ How long have you owned your pet?
✔ When did you first notice the problem?
✔ Does your pet appear to be in any discomfort or pain?

✔ What, if anything, have you given to your mouse or done to treat the problem?
✔ When did your mouse last eat or drink?
✔ Has there been a change in your pet's diet or living environment (change in bedding material)?
✔ When did your mouse last have a bowel movement?
✔ Does your mouse have normal stools, or constipation, or diarrhea?
✔ Is there any staining or caked feces around the anus or perineum?
✔ Are there any other animals at home? If so, what kind and how many?

Basic Requirements for Mice

✔ Fresh food and water.
✔ Clean, comfortable housing.
✔ Stress-free environment.
✔ Some degree of control over its environment, such as places to hide to avoid bright lights.
✔ Ability to express normal mouse behavior—resting, grooming, hiding, gnawing, social interactions.

✔ How many animals are housed in the same cage with your sick mouse?

✔ If you have other pets, did you purchase any of them recently?

✔ Do any of your other pets have any problems that seem similar or related?

✔ What do you feed your mouse (including special treats)?

✔ How is your mouse housed?

✔ What is the cage-cleaning schedule?

✔ Has your pet been exposed to any sick animals or chemicals?

✔ Where did you obtain your pet?

✔ If your mouse is a female, is it pregnant or when did it last produce a litter?

✔ Add any other findings or relevant information.

CHECKLIST

Essentials of Good Mouse Care

1 Good, nutritious food and fresh water
2 Plenty of space to run and play
3 Clean, dry, draft-free housing
4 Comfortable temperature and humidity
5 Nesting material and nest box
6 Chew toys to keep teeth healthy
7 Exercise wheel
8 Interesting toys
9 Another mouse to keep it company
10 Lots of attention from you

Health Problems

Because of their small size, mice are difficult to examine and medicate. They also seldom recover from serious diseases or injuries. The most important mouse health care you can provide for your pet is preventive health care.

Mice can contract a variety of bacterial, viral, and fungal infections. They may be troubled by external (skin, hair, ears) and internal (intestinal) parasites. Mice may also suffer from noncontagious medical conditions, such as cancer and genetic disorders.

A sick mouse looks ruffled and acts dull. The bright, alert look is gone. It does not want to eat, play, or be handled.

Skin, Muscle, and Skeletal Problems

Signs of skin problems include loss of fur, sores, dry, flaky, itchy skin, and moist, oozing, reddened skin. Skin problems may be caused by bite wounds, tiny skin parasites, allergies, hormonal imbalance, improper diet, disease,

or fungal and bacterial infections. Your veterinarian should diagnose the exact cause of your pet's condition. Often, a specific prescription medication is required to treat the problem successfully.

Bite wounds: Bite wounds are one of the most common types of injuries that occur in mice. You can reduce the incidence of bite wounds in your mouse colony by housing only compatible animals together, separating aggressive animals and housing them separately, not housing males together, and not overcrowding animals. Bite wounds can become infected and form abscesses. They are most commonly found around the rump and scrotum.

Because mice have such sharp teeth, bite wounds can be a serious injury. Deep puncture wounds frequently become infected and form abscesses. It is not uncommon for mice to die of serious bite wounds.

To check your mouse for bite wounds, push the fur back with your fingers and look for any

An active, playful mouse is a healthy mouse. If your pet loses interest in social activities, it is a sure sign that it doesn't feel well.

lumps, bumps, puncture holes, swelling, redness, tenderness, or pus. If a bite wound is deep, it can cause muscle and nerve damage.

Prevention: House only compatible animals together.

Treatment: Clean the wound with a mild antiseptic solution or hydrogen peroxide. Keep the wound clean and allow it to drain until it has closed on its own and healed.

Barbering: Dominant mice will bite or chew on lower-ranking mice, creating patches of hair loss on the skin (without skin lesions). Hair is usually missing around the muzzle, face, or neck. The dominant mouse can be identified because it seldom has any bald areas.

Prevention: Separate mice and remove the dominant animal from the colony, if necessary.

Ringtail: This is a rare problem in mice, caused by dryness (humidity below 50 percent). It occurs in preweaning and infant mice and is typified by circular constrictions around the tail and, rarely, the limbs, leading to gangrene and loss of the tail.

Prevention: Keep humidity at 50–55 percent in the mouse housing area.

Pododermatitis: Pododermatitis is more common in large animals but does occur in mice. It is an inflammation of the feet due to housing on hard wire-mesh floors.

Prevention: House your mice directly on soft bedding material.

Fungal diseases: Mice are susceptible to several types of skin fungi, including *Trichophyton* and *Microsporum*. These fungal infections are characterized by small areas of hair loss and scaly skin. Although these conditions can be contagious to humans, pet mice that are affected usually have contracted the disease from children that have ringworm!

Treatment: Prescription medication from your veterinarian.

Parasites: Mice can be infested with a variety of skin parasites, including mites and, rarely, fleas. Lesions are due to scratching and are usually located on the back. Some species of parasites are contagious to humans (*Sarcoptes scabiei*).

Treatment: Prescription medication from your veterinarian.

Respiratory Problems

Nasal obstruction: Mice can get small particles of bedding or food lodged in their nasal passages. Because mice cannot breathe through their mouths, nasal obstruction can result in suffocation.

Pneumonia: If your mouse is having difficulty breathing or has a discharge from the nose, take these symptoms seriously. Your pet may have been exposed to dangerous germs, or to a damp, cold, drafty environment. Whatever the initial cause, your mouse could develop pneumonia. Signs of pneumonia also include lack of appetite, inactivity, weight loss, and head tilting (from ear infection associated with some disease organisms).

Pneumonia is caused by viruses, bacteria, mycoplasmas, stress due to sudden drops in temperature, cold drafts, or accidental inhalation of food and dirty bedding material. Depending on the cause, the disease may persist, the animal may recover, or treatment may be unsuccessful. Pneumonia is a serious disease. Even with medical treatment, it usually results in death in most mice.

Dental Problems

The outer surface of the incisors is harder than the inside material, so as your mouse chews, its teeth are constantly chiseled and sharpened. There are no nerves in the incisors, except at the base of the tooth where growth takes place.

If your mouse is very tame, and if you feel comfortable handling it, you can check its mouth regularly for dental problems. You can do this by holding it with one hand and gently lifting its upper lips with your other hand, revealing the front incisors. Never place yourself in danger of being accidentally bitten. If you prefer, your veterinarian can perform the dental examination for you.

Most dental problems can be avoided by providing safe chew toys and a balanced diet sufficient in calcium content, and by removing animals with dental problems from the breeding program.

Malocclusion: When the incisors do not grow or align as they should, the teeth wear unevenly. This is called malocclusion and is usually an inherited problem. One or more of the misdirected incisors may grow into the roof of the mouth. This painful condition eventually makes it difficult or impossible for the mouse to eat. Signs of malocclusion may include lack of appetite, weight loss, palate trauma, and the presence of crumbled, uneaten food in the food dish.

Treatment: The offending tooth may be trimmed back. Although you can do this yourself using small animal nail clippers, you run the risk of accidentally fracturing the incisor. Your veterinarian can safely trim the tooth back using appropriate dental tools. No anesthetic is required, because there is no sensation in the upper part of the tooth. The dental tool is placed over the tooth and aligned where the cut is intended. If you elect to do the procedure yourself, check to be sure the tongue, lips, and cheeks are out of the way. If you feel uncomfortable doing this, ask your veterinarian to do it or to show you how.

The tooth will grow back and will need to be trimmed regularly. Mice that have dental malocclusion should not be used for breeding because this condition may be inherited.

Broken teeth: Sometimes an incisor may break. It will grow back, but during that time, the tooth opposite the missing or broken tooth may become overgrown because it has nothing to grind against. You may need to trim the opposite tooth until the broken tooth grows back.

Gum infection and tooth loss: Once in a while the gums may become infected and a tooth may need to be removed. Your mouse may have a swollen mouth and refuse to eat. Dental extraction is a job for your veterinarian!

Gastrointestinal Problems

Stomach and intestinal problems can be caused by bacterial or viral infections, parasites, improper diet, stress, or unsanitary housing conditions. These problems can cause constipation or diarrhea.

Constipation: Constipation—difficulty passing dry, hard feces—can be caused by dehydration, insufficient water intake, dry or hot environment, obstruction of the intestinal tract, and parasitism.

Treatment: Be sure your mouse can reach the water bottle and that the sipper tube functions properly. Remove all dry food and replace it with moist food, such as apple or lettuce, until the stools return to normal. Consult your veterinarian.

Diarrhea: Disease, infection, parasites, such as pinworms, and stress can all cause diarrhea and rectal prolapse. If not treated quickly, diarrhea can in turn cause rapid dehydration and even death. The feces are soft, mucous, or liquid and the anal area may be wet and soiled.

Treatment: If your mouse has diarrhea, it needs to be rehydrated and may need medicine to recover. Home remedies such as rice water may prove beneficial until you can contact your veterinarian for advice. Balanced electrolyte solutions may also help stabilize your pet's condition. Always make sure your mouse also has plenty of fresh water available at all times.

Rectal prolapse: Certain intestinal parasites, such as pinworms, can cause inflammation of the intestines. The intestines then swell and can protrude from the anus. The prolapsed rectum looks like a red tube sticking out of the body. This is a painful condition. If the swelling is not too great, the intestine can sometimes be gently pushed back into the body. Often, however, the intestine will prolapse again, shortly after it has been replaced. Treatment for rectal prolapse in mice is usually not successful.

Stress ulcers: Mice are easily stressed and can develop ulcers in the stomach and intestines associated with stress. Ulcers can lead to weight loss and poor health. If you suspect your mouse is suffering from ulcers, try to determine the cause and remove your pet from the source of stress. This may require isolating it from aggressive animals or loud noises, or providing it with more hiding places.

Nervous System Problems

Encephalitis: Mouse encephalomyelitis virus causes neurological problems, usually limited to paralysis of the hind limbs. No treatment exists other than making sure your mouse has plenty of food, water, and rest. If your pet is severely affected and cannot move about the cage, euthanasia is indicated.

Dehydration

Dehydration occurs when an animal loses too much water from the body. There are many causes of dehydration, including not drinking enough water, illness and diarrhea, and exposure to a hot, dry environment.

Treatment: The treatment for dehydration is rehydration, which is replenishing the body with water. When an animal becomes dehydrated, it also loses minerals from its body. If your pet is dehydrated, give it immediate

---

TIP

Homemade Solutions

Do not give your pet homemade salt or sugar mixtures without consulting your veterinarian. In the wrong proportions, these will do more harm than good by further dehydrating your pet.

---

access to fresh drinking water. Do not try to force water on your pet if it is unconscious or too weak to drink on its own, because it may aspirate the water into its lungs. Contact your veterinarian immediately and ask if a balanced electrolyte solution—a mixture of water and necessary minerals in the proper dilution for rehydration—is advised. Electrolyte solutions are available from your veterinarian. In an emergency, you can also find electrolyte solutions formulated for human babies, available at pharmacies and supermarkets. Keep a bottle on hand in case of emergency.

Ear Problems

It is difficult to tell if your mouse is having ear problems because it is difficult to see inside the ear canal. Ear problems may be caused by parasites, infection, or injury. Signs include scratching at the ears, head shaking, tilting the head to one side (torticollis), and loss of balance.

Treatment: Place a drop of mineral oil on a cotton-tipped swab and gently wipe away any dirt or debris from your mouse's ears. This may also give your pet some relief from itching. Your veterinarian can examine the cotton-tipped swab under the microscope to determine

Bright lights, loud noises, and overcrowding are stressful for mice. To prevent stress ulcers from developing in your mice, house them in a quiet area and give them hiding places.

bright. If there is foreign material in your mouse's eyes, or if they are dull, have a discharge, or are closed, you can flush the eye with a mild eyewash. Most eye problems are painful and exposure to light will make the pain worse. Place your mouse in a dark room and contact your veterinarian for an appropriate ointment or eyedrops.

Many eye problems look similar. For example, ulcers of the cornea and cataracts both give the eyes a cloudy appearance. Some eye problems cannot be treated or may be signs of additional health problems.

Treatment: Many eye conditions are very painful, and most require veterinary expertise, so make an appointment with your veterinarian immediately. Light will hurt your mouse's eyes so place it in a dark room until your veterinary appointment.

if the problem is due to infection or parasites. If that is the case, your mouse will need to have its ears cleansed and treated with a prescription medication. If your pet's condition appears to be painful, contact your veterinarian immediately.

Ear infections: Ear infections caused by *Mycoplasma pulmonis* can cause neurological problems such as walking in circles and torticollis (head tilting). Even with medication, torticollis usually persists and euthanasia is usually indicated because the animal cannot eat or drink.

Eye Problems

The most common eye problems in mice are eye injuries caused by bedding material lodging in the eye. The injured eye then becomes irritated and infected and very painful. Check your pet daily to be sure its eyes are clear and

Heatstroke

Unlike many animals, mice cannot pant and do not salivate to keep cool. By not panting and drooling, mice conserve precious body water. On the other hand, they heat up rapidly and will die at 98.6°F (37°C). If temperature change is sudden, mice can die at 78°F (25.5°C). Be sure that your mouse's cage is not in direct sunlight and is not close to any fireplaces or heaters. If you must transport your pet, never leave it in the car. On a warm day, a car can heat up to 120°F (48.9°C) in a few minutes, even with the windows partially open.

Adequate ventilation is also important to prevent your mouse from becoming too hot.

An animal suffering from heatstroke will quickly become weak, unresponsive, and eventually comatose.

Treatment: Realistically, it is virtually impossible to revive a mouse suffering from heatstroke. You can attempt to cool down your mouse by holding it in your hand in a sink of cool (not cold) water. Be sure to keep its head above water so it can safely breathe. If your mouse regains consciousness, dry it gently and place it in a dry, dark, comfortable cage to rest. Next, give your mouse a small piece of apple for moisture and provide it with plenty of water.

Injury and Trauma

Small animals have a way of often being in the wrong place at the wrong time. If your mouse is dropped, stepped on, attacked by the family dog or cat, or injured in any way, try to determine how seriously it is hurt. Isolate it in a clean, comfortable cage. Do not handle your mouse more than necessary. Observe it closely to be sure it acts and moves around normally and continues to eat and drink. Contact your veterinarian for advice.

Unavoidable Problems

Some medical conditions, such as problems with the heart, kidneys, liver, or other internal organs, may go unnoticed. Many problems associated with aging or genetics, such as diabetes or cancer, cannot be prevented. If your pet has a medical problem you cannot treat or cure, you can still provide the best home remedy of all—good food and a safe, comfortable, loving home.

Resistance and Sensitivity to Medications

Mice are resistant to some kinds of medications and sensitive to others.

Use only medicines prescribed for your mouse by your veterinarian and give no more than the recommended dose.

Warning: *Never give your mouse any medicine intended for you or your other pets.*

Zoonotic Diseases

Zoonotic diseases are diseases that can be shared between animals and humans. Many species of animals are carriers of certain diseases that do not make them ill, but can make people very sick. Likewise, people can carry germs to which they are resistant, but that adversely affect certain animal species. Some disease organisms cause illness in both humans and animals.

It is highly unlikely that your domestic mouse would carry any diseases that present a health risk to you. If your mouse becomes ill, your veterinarian can answer questions you may have about the contagion of different diseases or parasites.

T I P

Pinworms

You cannot contract pinworms from your mouse. The species that parasitizes mice (*Syphacia*) is different from the one that infests humans. Also, domestic pet mice that contract ringworm usually acquire it from infected children.

Mouse Health Check Sheet

Health Problem	Symptoms	Causes	Remedy	Prevention
Barbering	Patches of hair loss.	Dominant mouse bites and chews on others.	Identify dominant animal (the one without hair loss) and remove it.	House only compatible animals together.
Bite wounds	Sores, redness, swelling, infection, pain or tenderness, draining pus.	Fighting, overcrowding.	Cleanse wounds with antiseptic, peroxide; keep clean; allow to drain.	Do not overcrowd animals; remove aggressive animals.
Broken teeth	Tooth breaks and tooth opposite overgrows into mouth tissue, causing pain and inability to eat.	Trauma; chewing objects that are too hard.	Continue to trim tooth opposite broken tooth until broken tooth grows and both teeth mesh properly.	Do not allow the opposite tooth to grow into soft tissues of the mouth.
Cancer (tumors)	Most common form of cancer is mammary tumors; illness, lack of appetite, weight loss, depression, inactivity, sometimes visible lumps.	Old age, viral disease.	Keep pet comfortable; do not try to prolong animal's life if it is suffering.	Good nutrition may play a role in prevention of certain types of cancers.

Mouse Health Check Sheet (continued)

Health Problem	Symptoms	Causes	Remedy	Prevention
Constipation	Straining to pass hard, dry feces or inability to pass feces; depression; lethargy, hunched-up position, dry, ruffled fur.	Insufficient water intake, dehydration, heat, illness, intestinal obstruction, parasitism.	Make sure fresh water is available and within reach; offer a small piece of apple for moisture.	Keep mouse away from heat and areas of low humidity; provide water at all times.
Dehydration	Skin is stiff and lacks elasticity; when pulled it stands up and is slow to fall back in place; animal is lethargic and weak.	Bacterial or viral infections and diseases, stress, improper diet, heatstroke.	Remove from heat or area of low humidity, if applicable, and offer fresh water.	Make sure fresh water is available at all times.
Dental malocclusion	Protruding or misdirected front teeth, lack of appetite, inability to eat, weight loss, swollen, painful mouth, infection.	Possibly inherited condition; may also be due to trauma or injury.	Use animal nail clippers to trim teeth back to correct and even length; check and trim teeth regularly for mouse's entire life.	Do not use in breeding program.
Diarrhea	Soft, mucous, or liquid feces, odor, wet around anus, dehydration, lack of appetite, weight loss, lethargy, hunched-up position.	Can be caused by parasites (pinworms), infectious agents, stress, improper diet.	Pinworms can be treated with prescription medication. Isolate sick animals from other pets, offer fresh water to rehydrate; contact veterinarian to determine cause.	Provide proper nutrition and sanitary housing; do not stress.

(continued on page 78)

Euthanasia

When It's Time to Say Good-bye

Even with the best care in the world, your mouse will some day develop signs of old age or illness. This will be a difficult time for your pet, because it will not be able to play, socially interact, and enjoy life as it did when it was younger and healthy. It will also be an emotionally painful time for you, because you will feel helpless in your inability to prevent or cure the problem, and you will not want your small friend to suffer for a moment. At some point in time you will ask the question: Should my pet be euthanized?

Euthanasia means putting an animal to death humanely, peacefully, and painlessly. There are different ways veterinarians euthanize animals, depending on the circumstances. Euthanasia is usually done by first giving the animal a sedative to make it sleep deeply, and then giving it a lethal substance by injection that ends its life almost instantly.

If you are asking yourself whether your pet should be euthanized, there must be good reasons. The decision of when to euthanize is a difficult one that depends upon many things. Here is a good rule of thumb: If your pet's suffering cannot be relieved, or if your pet's quality of life is poor, or if the "bad days" simply outnumber the "good days" for your pet, it is time to seriously consider euthanasia. Your veterinarian can answer any specific questions you or your family may have.

During this emotional time, remember to take care of yourself and allow time to grieve. If you have children in the family, deal with the issue of animal loss at a level they can understand, comfort them, and let them share their grief (see Children and Mice, page 26). Take comfort in the knowledge that you took good care of your pet throughout its life and that you made the best decisions regarding its health and welfare, even when you had to make the most difficult decision of all.

The most common eye problem in mice is caused by particles of bedding material becoming lodged in the eye. If your pet's eyes are injured, they will be extremely sensitive to the light, so keep your mouse in subdued light and contact your veterinarian for advice.

Bright eyes and a glossy coat are signs of a healthy mouse.

Mice are most active during the evening.

Mouse Health Check Sheet (continued)

Health Problem	Symptoms	Causes	Remedy	Prevention
Ear problems	Scratching, head shaking, loss of balance, pain.	Parasites, infection, injury, disease.	Determine cause of problem to treat appropriately.	Avoid exposure to sick animals with contagious diseases.
Eye problems	Discharge, closed or dull eyes.	Bedding material lodged in eye, irritation, infection, and disease.	Flush eye with mild eyewash; treat with eyedrops or ointment; place mouse in a dark area; isolate from other animals.	Avoid using sharp bedding material; check animal's eyes daily for signs of problems.
Heatstroke	Hot, weak, unresponsive, comatose; appears to be dead.	Change in temperature, especially rapid temperature changes; inadequate ventilation.	Remove from hot area; submerge body in cool water while keeping head above water; dry well and offer fresh water.	House your pet at room temperature; do not house your pet at temperatures above 72°F (22.2°C).
Infections	Symptoms vary according to organism and type of infection.	Bacteria, viruses, fungi, protozoa.	Consult your veterinarian; do not allow problem to progress or animal to suffer.	Avoid exposure to sick animals that may have contagious diseases.
Rectal prolapse	Red, swollen tube-shaped tissue protruding from anus; lack of appetite; lethargy.	Intestinal parasites (pinworms).	Swollen tissue may be gently pushed back into the anus; this is not always successful, and rectum may prolapse again.	Medicate for intestinal parasites when present.

Mouse Health Check Sheet (continued)

Health Problem	Symptoms	Causes	Remedy	Prevention
Respiratory problems	Difficulty breathing, discharge from nose, lack of appetite, inactivity, weight loss.	Viral, fungal, or bacterial infection, exposure to cold, stress, nasal obstruction.	Isolate from other pets and allow time to recover; do not stress.	Avoid sudden changes in temperature, cold drafts, and exposure to sick animals with contagious diseases.
Ringtail	Annular constrictions around tail and limbs of infant mice, resulting in gangrene.	Low humidity.	Circular constrictions will not go away; amputation may be required.	Keep humidity in mouse area between 50 and 55 percent.
Skin and fur problems	Loss of fur, sores, flaky or moist skin, redness, oozing, itching, scratching, infection.	Bite wounds, bacterial or fungal infections, parasitism, improper diet, disease.	Contact your veterinarian for diagnosis and medication; keep skin and fur clean.	Avoid contact with animals infested with parasites; provide good nutrition; house only compatible animals together.
Stress ulcers	Weight loss, lethargy.	Stress.	Remove source of stress (noise, aggressive cagemates).	Keep stress to a minimum.
Trauma	Inactivity, lack of appetite, inability to walk or sit normally, broken bones, bleeding, swelling, pain.	Numerous possiblities, including being dropped, stepped on, or bitten.	Observe closely to determine extent of injury; isolate from other pets; contact veterinarian.	Make sure your pet cannot escape from its cage; house only compatible animals together.

RAISING MICE

Raising mice is relatively easy. It is also a lot of fun. But you will encounter some challenges along the way and there are some important facts you must know to be successful at your new hobby.

Reproductive Characteristics

Females: The female mouse has ten nipples and a bicornate uterus. That means that from the cervix, the uterus branches into a Y-shape, consisting of a left and a right uterine horn. This conformation enables the mother to carry several offspring in each of the elongated uterine horns.

All female mammals are born with a vaginal membrane that remains closed until puberty (sexual maturity) is reached. In mice, it opens a few days before the first estrus occurs.

Males: The testicles of mature male mice are contained in the scrotum and readily visible.

Upon ejaculation (the release of sperm during breeding), the secretions of reproductive accessory glands and the prostate gland mix with the semen. This gelatinous mixture forms a small plug, called a "copulatory plug," that prevents leakage of semen from the vagina. The copulatory plug is visible at the entry to the female mouse's vagina for about 24 hours after

Nature is full of surprises! This mother snuggles with her pups—every one is different and not one looks like her!

breeding, then it falls out and can sometimes be found in the bedding. It is a useful indicator that mating has occurred.

The Reproductive Cycle

Puberty

Female mice reach sexual maturity at six weeks of age; male mice reach sexual maturity between six and eight weeks of age.

Estrus

Mice are polyestrous. This means that they come into estrus more than once in a breeding season, which is essentially year-round for mice in captivity. The estrous cycle of mice is divided into proestrus, estrus, metestrus, and diestrus phases. Estrus occurs on average every four to six days, although there is a range of variation between mouse strains. It is the time period just before and just after ovulation and usually takes place at night. Some male mice will breed females when they are not in estrus and are not receptive. No litters will result from matings that

Mouse Reproduction Chart

Puberty	6-8 weeks
Estrous cycle	Polyestrous
Duration of estrous cycle	4-5 days
Gestation	19-21 days
Post-partum estrus	Yes
Average litter size	4-12 pups
Birth weight	.035-.65 ounce (1-1.5 g)

occur outside of estrus. If a nonfertile male breeds a female, pseudopregnancy (false pregnancy) can result, lasting 10 to 13 days before the female returns to estrus.

Within 24 hours of giving birth, the female mouse will come into estrus again. This is called a post-partum estrus. This early estrus is not uncommon in rodent species. Mice will breed and conceive on their post-partum estrus, which lasts 12 to 18 hours. Fertility is less on post-partum estrus than regular estrus and resulting litter sizes are often smaller.

Ovulation

Ovulation is the release of eggs from the ovaries. Mice are spontaneous ovulators, meaning they do not have to be bred in order to ovulate. Assuming the male is fertile, the number of young conceived will depend upon the number of eggs released during ovulation, and usually range from 4 to 12.

Breeding Behavior

Mouse reproduction and behavior is influenced by olfactory, visual, tactile, and auditory stimuli of other mice. Pheromones in urine are particularly important in allowing animals to recognize partners and identify receptive females. The male recognizes a female in estrus by olfactory cues and by her behavior. If the female is receptive, she will allow the male to sniff her and investigate her genital area. She will respond by assuming a position of lordosis, a posture in which she braces her legs and holds her back flat. It does not take long for the male mouse to begin breeding. He will make multiple mountings and breed the female several times over a period of 5 to 20 minutes.

Breeding Systems

Three main systems are used to breed mice: the monogamous system, the polygamous system, and the harem system.

✔ In the monogamous system, one male and one female are paired and housed together.

✔ In the polygamous mating system, one male is housed with two to five females in a large cage. Once the females become pregnant, they are removed from the group cage and housed separately, so they are not bred on their post-partum estrus.

✔ The harem system varies from the polygamous system in that the pregnant females are left in the cage with the male so they breed on their post-partum estrus, thereby producing more litters, although fewer offspring than usual may result from this breeding.

As always, pheromones play an important role in these breeding systems. It is very important that you do not place a pregnant female in with a strange male within the first five days after breeding (the pre-implantation phase), as this can cause the pregnancy to be blocked and the female to return to estrus within four to five days. The only time pheromones from a strange male will not block a pregnancy within five days after mating is if the female is currently nursing a litter, in which case her pregnancy will continue unharmed.

Be sure to record the date the breeding took place and mark the anticipated birth date on your calendar. You won't have long to wait—the pups will arrive before you know it, so be sure you have homes lined up for them in advance.

Pregnancy

Once a fertile mating has occurred, fertilization of the eggs (ova) takes place. The fertilized eggs grow into embryos and move from the mother's oviducts into her uterus. Five days after fertilization, the embryos attach to the wall of the mother's uterus. This process is called implantation; it enables the embryos to develop into fetuses. Each fetus receives its nutrition for growth through its umbilical cord, which is connected to the placenta, an organ that joins the mother and the unborn offspring during pregnancy. Each placenta is individually implanted in the wall of the mother's uterus.

The length of pregnancy, or gestation, is 19 to 21 days. It includes the time period from conception, when the female becomes pregnant, to parturition, when she gives birth.

Delayed Implantation

If a mother mouse already has a litter of three or more pups that she is nursing, and if she is heavily lactating, implantation of the embryos of the new litter can be delayed several days so that gestation may appear to extend up to 36 days.

Birth

Birth usually occurs between midnight and 4:00 A.M. There may be a slight vaginal discharge present a few hours before parturition. The mother mouse will begin making pronounced stretching movements one to two hours before the pups are born. At the onset of birth, she begins to clean her genital area. She sits up and crouches over to deliver her first-born pup, which may be born headfirst or tail first (breech). She licks the pup clean of birth membranes and blood, and separates it from the placenta by chewing the umbilical cord. She then eats the placenta. Any pups that are stillborn are also eaten.

For many animal species, the placenta provides nutrition for the mother when she is nursing her young and is unable to leave them alone to search for food, but mice have everything planned in advance. They almost always have more food stored than they will be able to eat.

Sometimes the pups are eaten along with the birth membranes and the placenta. Cannibalism is common and happens most frequently during the first week after birth, with mice that are first-time mothers or that are nervous, stressed, or upset.

Care of the Pups

Mother mice make a small depression in their bedding for the pups, usually located in a corner of the cage. The pups are born hairless and blind. They find their mother's nipples by using their sense of smell. Pheromones are secreted by the skin on the mother's belly and lead the pups to the nipples. Resist the temptation to handle the small, pink, hairless babies, as this intrusion will upset the mother. She must be left completely

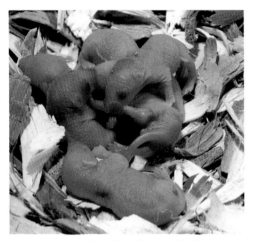

Mice pups are born hairless and helpless with their eyes and ears closed.

The mother huddles over her pups to nurse them and keep them warm.

alone; the slightest disturbance may cause her to eat or reject her pups. The mother may give birth to her pups in different areas of the cage, but she will eventually gather them up and place

Do not disturb the mother and babies. Mother mice can become upset and eat their young. This mother is standing guard over her newborn litter.

them all together in a nest. When she has finished having her babies, she will stretch and arch her back over the pups, while supporting herself on rigid legs. This is called *huddling.* It is the mother's way of covering her pups without crushing them. By huddling, she can keep her babies warm while they eat and sleep.

Pups should not be disturbed for at least two weeks. Be sure not to touch them with your bare hands. Your scent will cause the mother to reject her pups. If you absolutely do have to move the pups for some reason, wear vinyl gloves that have been moistened with urine in the cage bedding to reduce the likelihood of cannibalism by the mother. If you need to transport the pups to another cage, you can scoop them up in layers of bedding.

Litter Size

Litter size is influenced by the quality of diet the mother receives, as well as photoperiod, environmental temperatures (increased temperatures cause a decrease in fertility), embryonic mortality, genetics, and whether breeding took place on a post-partum estrus. Larger females tend to have larger litters. The first litter is usually the smallest. The fourth and fifth litters are often the largest. After six to seven months of age, litter size begins to drop. Female mice usually stop breeding after they have reached one to one and one-half years of age. (Males stop breeding at an older age than females.)

Lactation

Lactation is the production of milk by the mammary glands, or breasts. The composition of milk, its percentage of fat, protein, and water varies for each species. Lactation is a unique feature of all mammals. It makes it possible for mother animals to nourish their immature young safely in hiding, anytime, anywhere. It is a practical approach to increase survival of offspring during times of food shortage. Mice lactate for three to four weeks.

If the mother senses her pups are in danger, she will move them to a new location.

As the pups grow, they tend to wander from the nest and the mother spends a lot of her time retrieving them.

When a mother is lactating, she is turning the food she has eaten and the fat she has stored into milk for her babies. This process requires energy and burns up calories. It makes it necessary for the mother to eat more food and drink more water than usual. In fact, when she is lactating, a mother mouse will drink twice the amount of water, or more, than she usually drinks.

Mice produce body heat when they lactate. This body heat helps keep the pups warm. Mother mice may lose weight during lactation. Be sure to provide lots of nutritious food and plenty of water during that time.

Weaning

A weaned animal is an animal that no longer requires and is no longer receiving nourishment from its mother's milk. Baby mice should not be weaned from their mother earlier than three weeks of age.

Baby Mice

Imprinting and Taming

Imprinting is what takes place when a very young animal sees another animal and immediately forms a close bond with it. In the wild, baby animals imprint on their mothers. She is the first thing they see, smell, hear, and recognize. They depend on her for protection. They follow her and learn from her. The same is true for mice in captivity. By the time you are able to safely handle the babies, they will have already imprinted on their mother.

This in no way interferes with your ability to tame your baby mouse. Baby mice are gentle and tame. Frequent, gentle handling will keep it that way.

Sexing the Baby Mice

It is not difficult to determine the sex of the baby mice at an early age. Hold the baby carefully, belly up, with its back against the palm of your hand. You may hold the tail gently, but do not pull on it. The nipples on the female mice are very evident. In addition, the distance between the anus and the urethral orifice, or the anogenital distance, is greater in males than in females. By comparing the littermates to each other and noting the anogenital distance, you will quickly learn to identify the males from the females.

Identification and Record Keeping

Identification and record keeping are important aspects of a successful mouse breeding colony. The size and similarity in appearance of mice makes identification difficult. You will want to note which mice produce the largest, healthiest litters, and which mice are the most attentive parents. You will also want to keep pedigrees of the mice to keep track of the various color combinations you obtain in offspring from each breeding pair.

There are several methods of mouse identification; however, with the exception of microchips, there is currently no noninvasive method of permanently identifying them.

1. Cage cards. The cards remain attached to the home cage in a special card holder. The group card indicates the number of mice in the cage, their sexes, dates of birth, and identifying marks or colors. A separate card can be maintained for each individual animal's breeding record, showing date of breeding, date of parturition, number of pups in a litter, and the number of live pups at weaning. You may want to note other items of interest, such as the animals' colors, weights, and temperament. If you document a lot of information about your mice, you will probably prefer to use a notebook with a page assigned to each animal.

2. Marking pens. Mice can be marked on the tail with nontoxic marking pens. The identification mark will usually last two to three weeks and will need to be remarked regularly.

Mouse Development Chart

Age		Weight
Birth	Hairless; eyes and ears closed.	.035 ounce (1 g).
4 days	Ears open.	
7–10 days	Fully haired.	
10 days	Incisors erupt.	
14 days	Eyes open.	
21 days	Able to hear.	
21–28 days	Weaned.	$1/4$ to $2/5$ ounce (8–12 g).

3. Hair clipping. Small amounts of hair can be clipped from certain areas of the body as a form of identification. The hair will grow back in two to six weeks, so the clipping must be repeated regularly.

4. Hair dye. Nontoxic hair dye can be used in small amounts on specific areas of the body as a form of identification. Hair dye generally lasts longer than hair clipping.

5. Microchips. Microchips are the best method of permanent identification, but also the most expensive. Tiny electronic implants are placed under the skin by injection. Each microchip contains a unique identification code detectable by an electronic reading device. Microchips are a foolproof method to positively identify animals and are used extensively in research laboratories where animal mix-ups cannot be risked. If you are seriously considering raising large numbers of fancy mice and accurately tracking their genetics, microchips may be a good option for you.

For humane and esthetic reasons, other methods of identification, such as tattoos and ear notching, are less appealing to the mouse fancier. Fortunately, toe removal for identification is now discouraged and no longer commonplace.

Raising the Babies

Once you wean the young mice, they can be housed just like the adults. They have the same needs: nutritious food, fresh water, an exercise wheel, interesting toys, comfortable temperature, safe, escape-proof housing, and lots of attention.

Regular handling is an important part of keeping your pet tame. Young mice are naturally friendly. They are also curious and love to investigate. Your mice will be a continual source of fun and entertainment for you, and the more time you spend with them, the tamer and easier to handle they will be.

The Babies Leave Home

As tempting as it is, you will not keep every baby mouse you raise. As a responsible mouse breeder you will be sure that the youngsters are going to homes where they will receive good care.

✔ Provide the new owners with as much information as you can about their care.

✔ Show them the type of cage you use to house your mice.

✔ Demonstrate how to pick up the animals and examine them.

✔ Give the new owners a bag of the food you are currently feeding. This will prevent the stress of a sudden change in diet.

✔ Remind the new owners that travel is stressful for mice. They should transport the animal in a covered cage to protect it from bright light and loud noises. Remember to remove the water bottle from the cage during transport so it does not leak. A piece of apple in the cage will provide moisture until they arrive home.

✔ Recommend any veterinarians you know who have a special interest in pocket pets.

Try to encourage the new owners to take weanling mice from the same litter, so that they will be compatible. The mice you place in homes should have a minimum of five days to acclimate to their new surroundings and should be kept isolated from other mice in the new home for two weeks. Before they are introduced into a cage containing strange mice, the cage should be cleaned and bedding replaced with new so that the young mice are not attacked by the residents of the "home cage" or perceived as intruders.

BREEDING FANCY MICE

By now you have gained quite a bit of knowledge about mice, so you are ready to meet the challenges of detailed coat color genetics and breeding and exhibiting fancy mice.

One of the most exciting aspects of raising fancy mice is discovering the various types of color combinations that can be created through selective breeding. With a basic knowledge of genetic inheritance, a review of color genetics, and some perseverance, you can produce some very fancy mice. To achieve the color results you want, you must start out with animals that are carrying the genes for the specific colors and patterns you wish to produce. You will have a wide selection of colors to choose from when you buy directly from a mouse breeder, especially one that exhibits fancy mice and is active in mouse clubs and shows.

Color Genetics

Genetics and coat color inheritance in the mouse are topics that would fill an entire book;

Color genetics are fun! When you raise mice you can obtain colors ranging from basic brown (the color of most wild mice) to albino, Siamese, silver, lilac, chocolate, champagne, and more!

indeed, there are many books available that contain detailed information on these subjects (see Information, page 91). We will review the basics and describe some of the mouse colors currently recognized.

✔ The color of the fur and eyes are determined by the genetic makeup of the mouse.

✔ Half of the mouse's genetic material comes from its father, the other half from its mother.

✔ For each mouse trait, there are at least two genes, one inherited from each parent, that determine what the mouse will be like. Often, several genes are responsible for a specific trait. The genes interact in such a way that characteristics may or may not be observed in the individual mouse, yet may be present in its genetic makeup, able to be passed on to later generations.

Depending on how genes for particular traits are expressed, they are called *dominant*, *semi-dominant*, *recessive*, or *sex-linked* (traits that are genetically liked to the animal's sex). As you might imagine, dominant genes override the observable effects of recessive genes. Recessive gene traits are not evident unless the mouse has received the gene for the recessive trait from each of its parents. Semidominant genes produce effects that fall somewhere in between what you would expect from a dominant or recessive gene.

Let's say you want to produce a pup of a certain color and that this color is controlled by only two genes. If the desired color is inherited in a dominant fashion, only one parent needs to be carrying the gene for the specific color for you to have a good chance of producing some pups of that color. However, if the color you wish to produce is inherited in a recessive fashion, both parents must be carrying the gene in order to produce some pups of the desired color. A parent can be carrying the recessive gene for the color without actually being that color. This explains why, once in a while, you will find pups in a litter that are not the same color as either parent. It is likely the parents were each carrying a recessive gene for the color.

Inheritance of Coat Color

Fortunately for the color genetics enthusiast who enjoys a challenge, the inheritance of coat color is much more complicated. Color is often determined by the interaction of several genes. The genes that control eye color may or may not be linked to the genes responsible for coat color. To complicate matters, genes will some-

times mutate, or change. Many, if not most, mutations in nature have harmful, rather than beneficial, effects. But sometimes gene mutations result in new colors and patterns.

Wild mice come in basic brown and most laboratory mice are white or albino (white with pink eyes), but fancy mice come in many coat colors, including black, slate or blue, silver, red, fawn, beige, chocolate, lilac, and champagne. Popular coat patterns include agouti, argente, Siamese, Himalayan, sable, and roan. Fancy mice also vary in markings, coat lengths, and textures (flat sheen, satin sheen, frizzy, curly, long, short, or no hair at all). They vary in body types and temperaments. For example, English fancy mice have long bodies and tails, with very large ears and a calm demeanor. American fancy mice are rounder, with smaller ears and shorter tails and a busybody personality. Eye color is dark brown, black, or red.

Now that you are armed with information and enthusiasm, there is nothing to stop you from joining the ranks of mouse fanciers worldwide who dedicate their efforts to a hobby they love. These are the people responsible for the continued popularity and enormous success of the fancy mouse. You're in good company!

INFORMATION

Organizations

American Society of Mammologists
H. Duane Smith, Secretary-Treasurer
Monte L. Bean Life Sciences Museum
Brigham Young University
Provo, UT 84602-0200
http://asm.wku.edu

American Veterinary Medical Association
1931 N. Meacham Road
Suite 100
Schaumberg, IL 60173-4360
(847) 925-8070
www.avma.org

American Fancy Rat and Mouse Association
Geri Hauser, Secretary/Treasurer
9230 64th Street
Riverside, CA 92509-5924
(909) 685-2350
(818) 592-6590 fax
e-mail: *rattusrat@hotmail.com*
www.afrma.org

American Rat, Mouse and Hamster Society
K. Barber, Newsletter Editor
950 Emerald Grove Avenue
Lakeside, CA 92040-3721
(619) 561-5505
e-mail: *karlab@sciti.com*

LITTLE MOUSE CLUB
Wanda Wilson, Membership Services
603 Brandt Avenue
New Cumberland, PA 17070
(717) 774-1778
www.littlemouseclub.org

Rat, Mouse and Hamster Fanciers
Joyce Starkey, Secretary
2309 Country Ranch Drive
Modesto, CA 95355
e-mail: *jstarkey@telis.org*
www.ratmousehamster.com

Rat and Mouse Club of America
13075 Springdale Street
Suite 302
Westminster, CA 92683
(949) 722-5350
e-mail: *mgazette@aol.com*

Additional Reading

Foster, H. L., J. D. Small, J. G. Fox. *The Mouse in Biomedical Research*. San Diego: Academic Press, 1983.

Guttman, H. N. *Guidelines for the Well-Being of Rodents in Research*. Research Triangle Park: Scientists Center for Animal Welfare, 1990.

Laber-Laird, K., M. M. Swindle, P. Flecknell. *Handbook of Rodent and Rabbit Medicine*. New York: Elsevier Science, 1996.

Searle, A. G. *Comparative Genetics of Coat Colour in Mammals*. London, UK: Logos Press Limited, 1967.

Silvers, W. K. *The Coat Colors of Mice*. New York: Springer-Verlag, 1979.

This tricolor mouse is orange on white and shaded with dark hairs.

The cobby black and tan is recognized by its tiny ears and glossy black, robust body. Its underside is light tan.

Safe and sound! There's no place like home!

Feeding this fast-growing litter is hard work. This mother needs a quiet place to rest, lots of water, and plenty of nutritious food.

A variety of snacks and some rodent blocks make mealtime interesting.

Baby mice grow up fast. Enjoy them while you can!

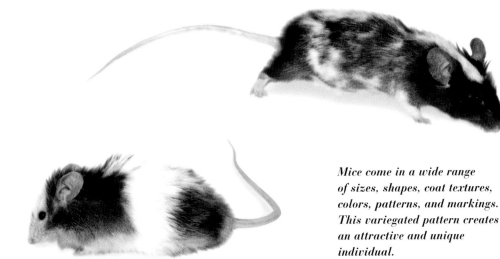

Mice come in a wide range of sizes, shapes, coat textures, colors, patterns, and markings. This variegated pattern creates an attractive and unique individual.

Longhair mice are very popular. This longhair banded tricolor (black, tan, and white) is as charming as it is cute!

About the Author

Sharon Vanderlip, D.V.M., has provided veterinary care to exotic and domestic animal species for more than 20 years. She has written books and articles in scientific and lay publications. Dr. Vanderlip served as the Associate Director of Veterinary Services for the University of California at San Diego School of Medicine, has worked on collaborative projects with the Zoological Society of San Diego, has owned her own veterinary practice, is former Chief of Veterinary Services for the National Aeronautics and Space Administration (NASA), and is a consultant for wildlife projects. She is the recipient of various awards for her writing and dedication to animal health.

Photo Credits

Zig Leszczynski: pages 2–3, 4, 5, 8 bottom, 9 top, 12 top, 12 bottom left, 12 bottom right, 13 top, 13 bottom left, 13 bottom right, 16, 17, 24 top left, 24 top right, 24 bottom left, 24 bottom right, 25 top, 25 bottom, 28, 29, 32 left, 32 right, 33 right, 36, 37, 40 left, 40 right, 41 top, 41 bottom, 44, 45 top, 45 bottom left, 45 bottom right, 48 top left, 48 top right, 48 bottom, 49, 52, 56, 57, 60 top, 60 bottom left, 60 bottom right, 61 top, 61 bottom left, 61 bottom right, 64, 65, 68, 72, 76, 77 top, 77 bottom, 80, 81, 84 top left, 84 top right, 84 bottom, 85 top, 85 bottom, 88, 89, 92 bottom left, 92 bottom right, 93 top left, 93 top right; Norvia Behling: pages 8 top, 9 bottom, 33 left, 53; Sharon Vanderlip: pages 20, 21, 92 top left, 92 top right, 93 bottom left, 93 bottom right.

Cover Credits

All covers by Zig Leszczynski.

Acknowledgments

I would like to thank my husband, Jack Vanderlip, D.V.M., for his invaluable help as an expert consultant in laboratory and exotic animal medicine. His behind-the-scenes activities included obtaining scientific resources and critically reviewing the final manuscript. His active participation and encouragement contributed significantly to the quality of the manuscript.

A special thanks to our daughter, Jacquelynn, for her expert mouse-handling during photo sessions.

Thanks also to editor Mark Miele for his expertise and assistance.

All inquiries should be addressed to:
Barron's Educational Series, Inc.
250 Wireless Boulevard
Hauppauge, New York 11788
http://www.barronseduc.com

ISBN-13: 978-0-7641-1812-8
ISBN-10: 0-7641-1812-9

Library of Congress Catalog Card No. 2001025606

Library of Congress Cataloging-in-Publication Data
Vanderlip, Sharon Lynn.
  Mice: a complete pet owner's manual /
  Sharon Lynn Vanderlip.
    p. cm.
    Includes bibliographical references (p.).
    ISBN 0-7641-1812-9 (alk. paper)
    1. Mice as pets.   I. Title.
SF459.M5 V36   2001
636.9'353—dc21   2001025606

Printed in China

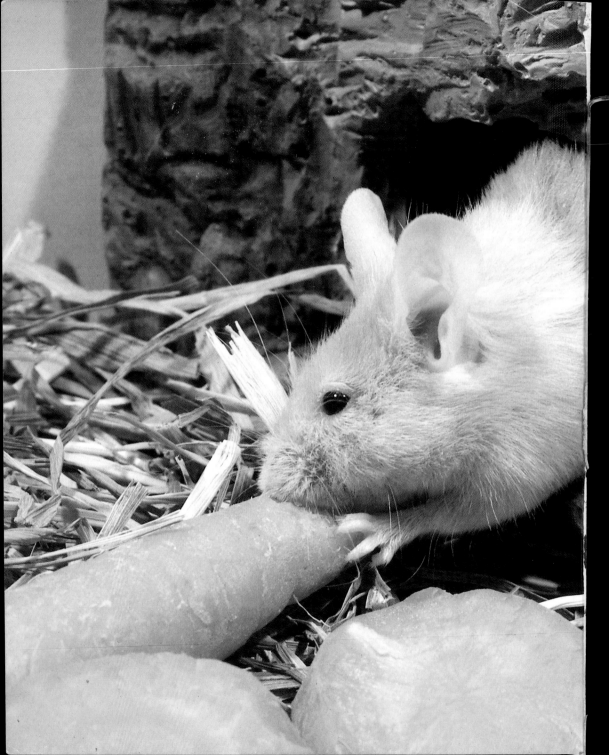